REV. JOSIAH OLUFEMI AKINDAYOMI
1909 - 1980

J. O. AKINDAYOMI:
THE
SEED
IN THE
GROUND

THE STORY OF THE FOUNDING
OF THE
REDEEMED CHRISTIAN CHURCH OF GOD

OLANIKE OLALERU

Father of Lights®
J. O. Akindayomi: **The Seed in the Ground**
Copyright © 2007 by Olanike Olaleru
Revised and Expanded 2012

ISBN: 978-978-931-229-0

Photographs with the assistance of:
Redemption Light Magazine
Pastor Ebenezer Ademulegun
Pastor Z. A. Mulero
Pastor Kolade Akindayomi and
Pastor (Mrs.) Funmilayo D. Olukowajo

Text setting in Goudy 13 points

Unless otherwise indicated, all scripture quotations in this book are taken from the **King
James Version** of the Bible

Christian Living/Biography

Published by
FATHER OF LIGHTS PUBLISHERS   for
FAITH OF OUR FATHERS FOUNDATION
208A Ikorodu Road Palmgrove,
Lagos, Nigeria.
0802-346-3141

Printed in Lagos Nigeria by
arimatheans@0802 318 5451

DEDICATION

THIS BOOK IS DEDICATED TO THE GLORY OF GOD and to every child of God in the world who believes in studying the history of the forbears and what learning our history means to the survival of the race.

Also to Roberts Liardon whose trail-blazing efforts in this area of ministry has been a tremendous inspiration.

ACKNOWLEDGEMENTS

MANY THANKS TO DADDY E. A. ADEBOYE who in his capacity as the General Overseer of The Redeemed Christian Church of God graciously granted permission for this all-important research work and also found time to write the Foreword.

We also appreciate Daddy's able P. A., Pastor A. A. Olorunnimbe.

Papa Akindayomi's children: Pastor (Mrs.) Olufunmilayo Durodoluwa Olukowajo, Pastor (Mrs.) Olubunmi Akindele, A/P Kolade Akindayomi, and Pastor Ifeoluwa Akindayomi; have been most kind, supportive and very helpful in all ways possible and imaginable to see this work to its successful completion.

We commend your commitment to Papa's memory.

Members of Rev. J. O. Akindayomi's extended family went the extra mile to make sure we lacked for nothing during the tedious field work. Thus we most gratefully appreciate Pastor Ebenezer Ademulegun who not only shared very intimate memories of Papa but also personally travelled to Ondo to take strategic snapshots of his beloved uncle's childhood home. Elder Wole Ogunsakin, another of Papa's nephews also gave useful hints and suggestions, apart from sparing time to talk about his times with Papa. Pastor J. A. O. Akindele (*Papa's son-in-law*) spent precious time to share great insight about Papa and the early days of the Redeemed Christian Church of God. We thank you all.

We most heartily appreciate Pastor Z. A. Mulero (*Papa's former driver*), and wife. Their arms and home were constantly open whenever we called. May the Lord reward you greatly. Pastor (Mrs.) Laide Adenuga of the International Office, Redemption Camp made initial contact arrangements. Thanks ma.

Our big daddy at Revelation Communications, Pastor Raphael Olatunji has always been there for us day or night, and in all ways. The Lord reward your large heart sir.

The staff of Redemption Light, especially Bro. Kola gave us tremendous support. We most sincerely thank Pastor Bowale Ajayi, daddy G.O's interpreter for his personal efforts to make sure this work sees the light of day.

Of course there are others too numerous to mention, but the sovereign Lord knows you and He will surely reward your kindness.

Finally in the tradition of the elders we salute the initial effort of Dr. Olusola Ajayi, DVM, author of Warrior of Righteousness, the first biographical work on Rev. J. O. Akindayomi.

You all have made the dream of **The Seed in the Ground** a reality.

CONTENT

FOREWORD

READING THIS MANUSCRIPT HAS GIVEN me deep satisfaction and delight. It is one more contribution to the body of literature about the founder and the foundation of The Redeemed Christian Church of God. An insightful and well researched work on how and why the RCCG has become what it is today and an assurance of its future.

This book should cause you to look beyond the glitz and glamour spreading around the Pentecostal Movement and soberly reflect on the significance of holiness, obedience, sacrifice, humility and faithfulness.

Reading **"The Seed in the Ground"** with *"Warrior of Righteousness"* will give you an overall grasp of the essence of the man - Pa Josiah Olufemi Akindayomi.

There are a number of important lessons which have been taught over and again in the Bible and the life and ministry of God's generals which are self evident in this book.

Do not despise the days of small things-Zachariah 4:10. RCCG could not have had a smaller and humbler beginning-Job 8:7 **"Though your beginning was small thy latter end should greatly increase"** -If you remain humble, holy and faithful.

It is sobering to note that Pa Josiah Akindayomi, with his passion for holiness, souls, righteousness, faithfulness and disinterest in the things of this world, was sent back from heaven to make some amendments before he was allowed in. If the righteous be scarcely saved where will the unrighteous be? A man's life does not consist of the abundance of his possessions!

Pa Akindayomi was on the move throughout his life and made constant adjustment as led by the Holy Spirit so much so that the man who passed on in 1980 bore only a slight resemblance to the man called in 1952. He was never sedentary and was always improving. A tree is known by its fruits. The fruits of the life and ministry of Pa Akindayomi speak for him and for themselves.

The encouraging message so eloquently demonstrated by Pa Akindayomi's life is that God can use anyone who is prepared to be a faithful covenant partner. God can use you. He will use you we pray. God bless you.

Pastor E. A. Adeboye
General Overseer
Redeemed Christian Church of God

PREFACE TO
THE REVISED EDITION

A S IT IS EXPECTED IN ANY WORK OF research that the last page is never closed as long as there is life, so has it happened to this worthy work on the phenomenal Christian mission called The Redeemed Christian Church of God. The book: **The Seed in the Ground** which chronicles the life and times of RCCG founder, Rev. Josiah Olufemi Akindayomi and how RCCG started, has been a work in progress since it was first published in year 2007.

With the co-operation of Papa's children, family members, pastors and associates, plus available documented materials, we worked with facts as we had them at the time. Shortly after public release of the book however, some of the readers who also happened to be eye-witnesses of some of the events came forward to corroborate some of the stories and also helpfully shed more light on some grey areas.

As a result we have therefore done a thorough review and editing of **The Seed in the Ground**, as you know it, making efforts to add and correct *(where necessary)* portions where we now have more accurate detail. It is very important to note that the book is essentially not different from the original publication, but just that some few grey areas have been clarified and new facts supplied. For instance we have material in Papa Akindayomi's handwriting where he stated his date of birth as 1909, whereas we had indicated that he was born in 1905.

Before the celebrated restitution with his second wife, we discover that he had done some form of restitution earlier before in his walk with God. While at Ile-Ife the Lord had sent Prophet Josiah back home to carry out some specific instructions, one of which was that he should send away a woman with whom he had been living without being married, back in Ondo. He said the Lord made him realise that the woman was *"a partner in sin."* This he did along with other instructions before returning to the C&S Movement at Ile-Ife.

Another area of great interest which we had reported on, and which seemed to have touched many Christian readers and made them to closely examine their walk with the Lord, is the issue of Papa's disagreement with the leadership of The Apostolic Church over the issue of some burnt tracts.

During our research for **The Seed in the Ground,**

nobody was able to tell us specifically how Papa came to include 'Apostolic' as part of the name of his church at this time, *(a title to which Apostolic Faith Church laid exclusive claims to)*, before God gave him the name Redeemed Christian Church of God.

Papa's translation of an Apostolic Faith Church tract from English to Yoruba for the purpose of evangelism, without prior permission from the Apostolic Faith leadership, and their taking exception to his use of 'Apostolic,' caused much trouble which in the long run, almost cost Papa Akindayomi his coveted place in eternity.

Over time, we have been able to unearth the facts about what actually transpired.

The details have now been included in this revised edition, thus properly piecing together a somewhat disjointed puzzle.

It makes interesting reading.

"And those twelve stones,
which they took out of Jordan,
did Joshua pitch in Gilgal.
And he spake
unto the children of Israel,
Saying,
When your children shall ask their fathers,
in time to come, saying,
what mean these stones?

Then ye shall let your children know,
saying, Israel came over this Jordan
on dry land"

Joshua 4: 20-22

INTRODUCTION

BEFORE YOU BEGIN TO READ THIS BOOK, let me tell you a secret: the strength and influence of the phenomenon known today as the Redeemed Christian Church of God, did not come by accident at all. True, it's a work of the Holy Spirit, but do you realise that the Holy Spirit does not work in a vacuum?

The Holy Spirit anoints faithful and humble vessels to birth God's purposes here upon the earth. And that's how great works get done for God. When you see a dimension of the power of God upon the earth, then know assuredly that the Holy Spirit had found a willing vessel which He was able to fill and possess fully.

For a great God-dream like Jesus to manifest upon the earth the Holy Spirit had sought for and found spacious accommodation in the young maiden called Mary who subsequently birthed the dream.

Eventually Jesus the Christ became the toast of kings, world rulers, great men, the poor and lowly alike. He became **"the desire of the nations"** (Haggai 2:7) as it were. Even hell could not remain the same simply because Jesus came. But then we could never forget that He was **"Jesus of Nazareth"** the humble Son of an obscure carpenter in a little village and the seed of a young woman who probably could not even read or write. Like her husband, the young Mary, mother of Jesus, was a peasant.

When great leaders in the Kingdom of God fall asleep, we owe ourselves the sacred duty of examining the quality of their faith in God which propelled them to where they got to before passing the baton, so that we can learn priceless lessons for our own lap of the race of faith. For beloved, it is a race and we all are running whether you realise that or not.

Before His final ascension the Lord appeared unto His disciples and said unto them by way of parting, **"And ye are witnesses of these things"** (Luke 24: 48).

The Lord had done things His disciples could point to and identify with for the rest of their lives. And indeed we also today are witnesses unto the acts of the fathers, because we have lived with them, watched their lives, observed their ways and seen how they lived **"holily and justly and unblamably"** before the Lord. The father of the faith, Abraham, did not become **"the father of the faithful"** (Romans 4: 16) overnight. There is the story of Abram the heathen from Ur of the Chaldees who took a series of journeys until he arrived where God gave him rest and the assignment to father a people for Him. We also are the fruit of that divine transaction. No tree grows from the top. There is always the story of how the seedling was first planted in the ground. The huge, big man you see today started one day as a tiny spark in the dark womb of his mother. God begins His big things in quite unsuspectingly small ways.

The Bible's famous *"Hall of Faith"* listed men and women whose brand of faith accomplished such naturally impossible feats that they caused a stir in the earth. And when you examine it closely you would discover that those supernatural feats were the first of their kind in each instance. A true apostolic ministry begins via a departure from the old pathways wherein God had identified errors (See Hebrews 8: 7-13). Here the former familiar, well known road maps will not work any more. Thus the man for the job *(of tracing the new pathways)* is often a man on the spot.

Alone, much misunderstood, set apart, and many times taken for an extremist-until God mercifully validates his call. For example, in the book of the generations of Adam, the first man on earth, we never heard that anyone walked with God until Enoch (See Genesis 5:22). Yet Enoch was the seventh man from Adam. But his willingness to walk a new route with God made all the difference. No one among Enoch's forebears ever told him about any holy God, yet we read that **"Enoch had this testimony, that he pleased God"** (Hebrews 11: 5b). Every apostle in every generation has always had some encounter with the sovereignty of God, which they determinedly work and run with. Thus they always walk away from the crowd and operate differently from the status-quo. The Bible elders were said to be men who ran on earth **"as seeing Him Who is invisible"** (see Heb. 11: 27), and that was the secret of their success.

Despite his background Enoch walked with God and with such diligence that he was separated from all others in a remarkable and distinctive manner. A woman like Sarah, said to be *"as good as dead"* for the deadness of her womb and more especially because *"she was past age"* of childbearing (See Hebrews 11: 11-12), was delivered of a healthy bouncing son at about age 90! Nobody ever had that kind of incredible story before - until Sarah. Why? It is written that Sarah **"judged him faithful who had promised."** God gave Sarah the understanding of an unusual possibility and she chose to hold unto God's word against all odds. If she failed she was willing to fail on God's side rather than on the side of natural thinking and reasoning. But that she succeeded made her truly to become the mother of a multitude of peoples, just as God had told her. And Sarai the barren, became Sarah, the mother of nations and kings.

What about Moses? He turned his back on an opulent kingdom and ended up becoming the father of a new nation under God. What happened? We read that Moses **"refused"** something and **"chose rather"** something else, because he saw beyond his immediate surrounding (See Hebrews 11:27). Moses' sight into the realm of existence beyond this earth propelled a kind of faith in him that could confront occultic powers and world monarchs. Moses was your example of a *"stubborn man,"* but with his hard faith he led millions of people through a dry wilderness on nothing else, but the word of promise from God. He kept telling them that God had a Promised Land waiting for them flowing with milk and honey, if only they would follow Him faithfully and keep His laws unto the end of that journey.

After the death of Moses the Hebrews indeed found themselves in the Promised Land that the man of God had told them about. Hidden in the acts of these men and women of old was the strength of the Almighty God which encouraged and emboldened them beyond the natural, despite terribly difficult prevailing situations and circumstances. Their labours into which we have freely entered today came at great personal costs. But they had tapped into the incredible power of God and thus changed each of their generations in a profound manner, thereby leaving behind great challenges for us. What they believed dictated how they lived and commanded their children and followers after them.

But you know what, beloved? You couldn't get their stories to read at all except God had appointed some faithful scribes to apply pen to paper. Recording the history of the race faithfully and accurately is a sacred responsibility in any civilization. As they say in the world, *"when you don't study history, and learn from it you become history yourself."*

Knowing the value of recorded history, especially for generations yet unborn, the Spirit of God had sovereignly moved on chosen vessels to diligently document these things for us. Thus today we have *(what is called)* the Bible. But for the invaluable ministry of writing we could not know about our father Abraham or mother Sarah nor indeed elder Moses, and all the others. Jesus Christ as Man had to have in-depth knowledge of the Books of the prophets. Before He ever stepped out into public ministry the Lord knew intimately what the prophets had said about God and His people, and indeed the whole world.

Suppose those things had not been recorded? Remember what the pompous Jewish teachers asked Him, having witnessed His deep knowledge and wisdom? (See John 7:15). True spiritual education comes from a rounded knowledge of the acts and exploits of our forebears-ancient and modern. We have these stories today to assure us beyond any reasonable doubt(s) that the living God is truly faithful and indeed **"a rewarder of them that diligently seek Him"** (See Hebrews 11:6).

To any one who would believe in Him, God is always the same yesterday, today and forever.

Rev. Josiah Olufemi Akindayomi whose life story we are about to encounter in this book, like his predecessors in the Scriptures, and in contemporary times never consciously set out to make a name nor create any remarkable impact anywhere. A humble man of very lowly beginnings and little means, Akindayomi just wanted to serve God as diligently as he understood how. He followed an inner voice he was able to recognise as the Almighty's; even though he never knew nor saw God before. But he constantly journeyed by Divine direction for several years, moving from this point to that until he was shown his place of rest.

That Papa Akindayomi followed not **"cunningly devised fables"** nor **"old wives' tales"** nor **"the unknown God"** is today apparent in the formidable oak known as the Redeemed Christian Church of God (RCCG), which he founded. In the light of what Akindayomi's little flock out at the stinking lagoon front in Ebute-Metta, Lagos has become today here at home and all over the world, one can only say that truly a prophet came into the Western shores of Nigeria at a time, and everything he said *"came to pass."*

In the words of Pastor J. A. O. Akindele, former A. G. O. (Admin. & Personnel) of RCCG; *"no one would have believed that a man who never even knew the way to the airport understood what he was talking about when he said his God told him that this church would become a worldwide phenomenon and that white people would even come from abroad to worship God there."*

It all started, Jesus said, as a single seed of wheat willing to fall unto the ground and die (see John 12: 24). Today, the mustard seed has budded under rain and shine plus the heat, and has blossomed into a great tree in the earth. The tree is grown and become strong with its height towering above many with its branches reaching unto the ends of the earth. That seed in the ground was a tiny mustard known in the natural as Josiah Olufemi Akindayomi, a.k.a "*Baba Alakoso.*"

I encourage you dear reader, to study the following account diligently and with an open heart. Expect to receive from the Lord knowledge, understanding and revelation for your own earthly journey and walk with God as you follow on to know the Lord; just as the humble, faithful and diligent servant of God, Rev. Josiah Olufemi Akindayomi did, and thus became a choice vessel in God's great house for his own generation and beyond.

Happy reading!
Pastor Olanike Olaleru
May, 2007
Lagos, Nigeria

"I am like a person going on a journey in a stagecoach, who expects its arrival hourly and often gets up and looks out of the window for it"
- John Newton (1725- 1807)
Author of *"Amazing Grace"*

CHAPTER ONE

PERSPECTIVES

B Y THIS TIME TOMORROW YOU ALL WILL *be giving glory to God in all Redeemed churches and thanking Him.*" All present said "*amen*" to the "*prophetic declaration,*" but never understood the meaning nor import of what they had just assented to.

Tomorrow was Sunday, yes, they would all surely be in church. They were family and close aides of the snow - headed old man lying full length on the bed.

Everyone standing around him, including the church prayer warriors and pastors had been praying fervently that "papa" would be on his holy feet once again and come to church to pray with them (*the man had such an unusual spirit of prayer*) or preach one or two of those his intent soul searching sermons again. Even to be present and sing one or two of those favourite songs of his would be just fine. When Papa sings he carried you straight from here to there:

> Mo n 'te s'iwaju l'ona na
> (I'm pressing on the upward way),
> Mo n 'goke si l'ojojumo
> (New heights I'm gaining every day;)
> Mo n 'gba'dura bi mo ti n 'lo
> (Still praying as I'm onward bound)
> "Oluwa f'ese mi mu 'le."
> ("Lord, plant my feet on higher ground")

Refrain:

> Oluwa jo gbe mi s'oke
> (Lord lift me up)
> Ki n' duro l'ori'le orun
> (And make me stand)
> T'o ga ju ile gbogbo lo,
> (By faith, on heaven's table land)
> Oluwa f'ese mi mu 'le.
> (A higher plane than I have found;)
> (Lord, plant my feet on higher ground)

By the time he was wending the accordion of his melodious voice heavenwards, not a soul in the congregation wanted to remain back here on earth. All wanted to follow the old man to that beloved heaven he never tired to talk and sing of.

But Papa was not singing nostalgically of heaven today, nor even exhorting the anxious band around his bed about the beauty of that land and why they must live holy in order to get there. The old man had just received the sure signal that by this time on the morrow he would be walking through those ancient pearly gates into his eternal rest and reward finally. The journey had been long and tedious, though eventful and colourful.

The labour of the labourer would soon come to an end and there would be no more longing for home. Home just beckoned that everything was now ready. The angels were waiting eagerly and joyously to receive him. What a relief and joy!

None present had the slightest idea of the intense spiritual transaction taking place between the man of God and his home country. They just knew Papa intermittently closed his eyes, opened them again, asked them what the time was and closed his eyes again. It seemed like eternity, but the man with the penetrating gaze of a seasoned prophet they all knew him to be, opened his eyes again and told his band of the faithful what would soon be hereafter, and sure as a gun everyone said "Amen!" Why not? Whatever Papa says always comes to pass. Why shouldn't they say amen? This prophetic utterance meant Papa would be on his feet again, sometime today possibly. His tired body that had known much fasting and hard training would be off the bed finally. Thus every one in church tomorrow would have reason to give glory to God and thank Him for restoring Papa to them. Or so they thought. But they were all wrong! Only Papa understood the meaning of his own declaration.

By the break of dawn on Sunday, November 2, 1980 the

founding father of the modest flock at No.1, Cemetery Street, Ebute Metta, Rev. Josiah Olufemi Akindayomi a.k.a. "*Baba Alakoso*" had crossed from this threshold unto eternity. Never to be seen or heard again in the physical, except through the legacy of his faithful hands left behind. And what a legacy!

What was left right now on the expansive bed in the solemn room were the remains of the unassuming, but tough Ondo man with a big God. He went away exactly as he had said it would happen.

Before finally breathing his last in the early hours of that glorious Sunday, Papa had said to those present with him, "*please draw up the covers very well and cover me properly right up to my feet.*" They promptly obeyed him. Then pointing his flashlight at the wall clock, he asked again, "*what time is it?*" He had done that throughout the night. It's as if he was expecting somebody or had an urgent appointment to keep somewhere. This time they told him it was past 4.00 a.m. It was Sunday morning already. Papa had his wish. He already said it long ago that he would never depart in the middle of the night because in his words "*only thieves move in the night.*" Thus this early dawn Papa turned on his side, ceased talking to anyone, closed his eyes and promptly slept off! The time was exactly 4.25am

Unknown to those who had kept vigil by the old man's bed through the night, he had been expecting his home-bound flight. Now it was here. Papa wasted no time at all. He instantly flew home in a triumphant hale. Therefore all his spiritual children must indeed go to church this morning like he had predicted yesterday; and go to give thanks to the Almighty who had faithfully seen Papa through. He was seventy-one years old.

A CURIOUS BEGINNING

Originally born Ogunribido Ogundolie, Rev. Josiah Olufemi Akindayomi the founder of what eventually became known as The Redeemed Christian Church of God, was born into a typically Ogun worshiping family in Ondo town in Ondo State of Nigeria. His father's house located at No. 12, Odo-Alafia Street, Odojomu area of Ondo had a prominent Ogun shrine located in the very centre of the courtyard; and every child in the compound was made aware that Ogun was the family god and protector.

Ogunribido, (*whose name translates: Ogun has found a place of abode*) took to the Ogun worship with his whole heart. A naturally single-minded individual, no one at home was in doubt that the young man would end up as a full fledged Ogun priest, as had been predicted to his father at the shrine that his son, Ogunribido would become *"God's servant."* And truly right from youth Ogunribido himself always knew in his heart that "God" wanted to use him. What he wasn't sure about was which God-the god of iron his fathers served or another God. He knew neither.

A striking feature about the young Ogunribido however

was that he was always different among his siblings. Nobody knew why but something about the boy made him distinct from all other children in the house. If he had any light at all, he probably would have recognised or suspected when he became a young man that he was destined to be about his heavenly Father's business and not that of Ogun, the god of iron. Secondly, the unusual zeal and fervour he exhibited in the service of Ogun, would have been recognised as the grace of the Almighty for him to serve the true and living God. But you see, God hardly does His things in obvious or familiar ways. Ogunribido Ogundolie even had a stint as a native doctor sometime before he finally encountered the Lord of glory.

WHAT WAS HOME LIKE?

Ogunribido's father who adopted his own father's first name-Akindayomi, was a titled Chief of the Ondo kingdom. He was the *Oloyinmi*. Oloyinmi, apart from being a committed Ogun worshipper was also a core traditionalist. He believed very much in the ways of his ancestors.

That his own curious son Ogunribido was fervent in the Ogun worship and service, therefore was quite pleasing to the old man. And since the gods had even predicted that the boy would end up as a servant of the gods, it was not a bad way how he was coming up. A practicing farmer, the Oloyinmi never bothered about sending his children to school. Thus Ogunribido, like his other siblings grew up not having any form of Western education. Farming was a family affair in those days. Whatever other occupation of the family head, the farm was where the heart was. The large number of children in a typical African household made farming the wise and practical choice.

Each family grew its own food and supplied the labour. Therefore no one in the family could be exempted and early morning was the time for farm work for the entire household. Everybody went to farm and worked hard, at least until about mid-day, as a rule. But somehow, young Ogunribido was not a 'normal' child in that sense. He could never fit into the traditional mould of going to farm and working like the others did. He went to farm quite alright, but never touched farm work. As soon as they all arrived the farm he conducted himself differently. While every one took to the day's work on the farm, Ogunribido went in another direction all by himself. He would find a cool spot under the shade of some tree, preferably with a log close by.

There he commenced his own self-appointed day's business of singing all the Christian (church) songs he knew. For the duration of the farm hours he got involved with no one else. When the day was over they all trooped back home together. Just as farming was a family affair, so also was the preparation of the evening meal- the main meal of the day comprising pounded yam and bush meat. While other children carried and fetched for the adults doing the cooking, Ogunribido was at another angle of the courtyard away from the busy scene. He would call young people like himself together and in the typical *"Aladura"* (Cherubim&Seraphim) fashion prevalent at that time, begin to lead them in prayer and songs.

Afterwards he would pray into water and instruct them to use it according to any ailments they had. Interestingly, the young man's prayers seemed to work for those he prayed for and it was reported that some even claimed that they were healed. Thus since his youthful days Ogunribido had earned the title of *Woli*, i.e prophet. It was also observed by adults around him that many things the young man said seemed to have a way of coming to pass. Members of his family were often left wondering at this weird one in their midst.

As a young man Ogunribido himself was said to have learned from his mother, Madam Olakuobi that right from his childhood, herself and his father always felt that there was something different about their little boy. For instance the grown up Akindayomi related how his own mother told him that since about age five, whenever he fell ill and any form of native soap *(ose dudu)* or juju medication was administered on him just like other children; he would never amend. Rather than get better his condition worsened. But if ordinary cold water was used to bathe him, all symptoms left, and he instantly began to improve. Why his own case was like that his parents had no idea.

Could this be a special child from God? But his parents

didn't know God! None among his father's forebears was known to have ever had a thing to do with the living God. Was he indeed a prophet of God in the making? No one at home knew and honestly none gave it a thought or allowed the boy's queer ways to bother them.

To the best of their knowledge, the young boy was just a lazy bones looking for any escape from the obvious rigours of farm work and the inconvenience of housework. None of the adults in his immediate family took any of his "church"activities to heart either. They expected that phase of youthful exuberance to pass with time. But somehow it did not pass away. The young man held his nightly 'crusades' regularly and he never lacked for a happy congregation. With time Ogunribido became quite popular for his "*isoji*" (i.e. Revival meetings) in the Odojomu quarters of Odo-Alafia area where his father's house was located. People in the neighbourhood continued to call him "*Woli*" (i.e prophet), mostly in a joking way. However the Almighty God did not seem to be joking. This was the foundation of something promising and quite exciting.

JOURNEY INTO LIGHT
Even though Ogunribido had been shown the way of Ogun, as the family's god since childhood, and he had served it most fervently, one day his real Owner and Maker came along and laid claim on him. Chief Oloyinmi his father, never thought that this unique one among his children could have served any other but their beloved god of iron, but his calculations didn't

quite add up. His belief that Ogunribido was somehow a set apart one was right, but his conclusions that it was to Ogun was way off the mark.

Around 1927, when Ogunribido turned 18, his natural hunger for God got him involved with the CMS *(now Anglican Communion)*. While there he told himself that he would give the Western education stuff a try, and here they started him with the equivalent of today's kindergarten, teaching him to read and write ABC. But it seemed the Oyinbo man's learning did not just agree with his star, because nothing they taught him stuck. Soon he abandoned the whole idea, and concentrated solely on his church membership. However while with the CMS, Ogunribido was taught some rudiments of the Christian faith, called catechism; baptised by immersion, and christened Josiah Olufemi.

In 1931, when Josiah was now 22, he left the CMS to join the obviously more vibrant and fervent Cherubim and Seraphim Movement church (C&S). This would be his home church for very many years to come and God would finally call him out to chart a new path into what is today known as the Redeemed Christian Church of God, but the journey was yet long and rather eventful.

Even though born and bred in an idolatrous environment Ogunribido somehow had always had an unexplainable pull in his heart towards God which often made him hungry for an encounter with the true God. This thirst, which he himself said had developed into a real pang, it was, that led him to join the CMS in 1927. But by the time he had spent some four years with the CMS he began to get agitated again; because despite his CMS membership and commitment Papa himself confessed later in life that: *"My thirst was not getting quenched and something kept nudging me that I was yet to hit the truth."* [1] This no doubt, was the beginning of God's sovereign move in young Josiah's life even without his own knowing.

A quite fortuitous incident became the final straw that broke Josiah's camel's back with the CMS, resulting in his sudden departure. Interestingly despite his CMS membership at this time Josiah was also a practicing herbalist (Babalawo). Now in the year 1931 he had gone to demand some money being owed him by one of his clients in town when the matter degenerated into a hot exchange of words. An elderly C&S prophetess who happened to be passing by got attracted to the scene and she tried to make peace between the two contenders. But Ogunribido would have none of that because collect his money he must; and that was the only thing he was ready to hear. The C&S woman wanted him to take things easy instead.

In frustrated annoyance Ogunribido released terrible vituperation on the peace maker and later followed it up by supernaturally sending a snake to harm her. Surprisingly no evil or bad report came back to him concerning his victim. In wonder Ogunribido a few days afterwards went in search of the C&S woman wishing to know what kind of power shielded her from his conjurations. They had a long talk. Afterwards Ogunribido renounced all his juju powers and herbal practice, made peace with God and would not go to the CMS again. He came under this prophetess' influence and began to follow her to her C&S church in Ondo. This woman it was who began to tutor Ogunribido in the things of the spirit.

Ogunribido particularly loved the C&S because it was given to the practice of fasting, dynamic prayer, visions and trances. In those days, the next best alternative to the conservative foreign orthodox churches around was the Cherubim & Seraphim (C&S) Movement founded originally by Prophet Moses Orimolade Tunolase, an indegene of Ikare in the old Western Nigeria.

Another major plus for the C&S those days was the fact that the worship was thoroughly African with vigorous clapping, dancing, heavy drumming, high praise and much show of emotion. The typical African religious inclination and tendency found strong expression with the Orimolade Movement therefore. For Ogunribido particularly this church was wonderful, because the language of communication was Yoruba. He found much satisfaction with the C&S and thus joyfully settled down here.

Some three years after joining the C&S, Josiah began to feel in his heart that God would want him to become a minister of the Gospel *(Ajihinrere)* . Now a young adult in his own right, and being without any education he had had to revert to farming as a profession, and he wasn't doing too badly. So how could God now ask him to leave his source of livelihood and become a minister? Josiah was not very happy about that kind of call at all, so he ignored it. But the strange feeling persisted to the point of distraction, and one day he decided to seek counsel with his superiors in church. His leader told him point blank: "*God needs you and He is calling you. Hearken quickly to God's voice.*" [2]

Even though Josiah resisted the call of God for good seven years, but God did not relent. Apart from the persistent voice of God, the reluctant prophet could never again do well at any venture he laid his hands upon. Nothing worked. He lost his peace, went progressively down, moving from one crop failure to another at every harvest season. Soon he faced total bankruptcy, and became completely helpless. When it became clear that God would not bend His own will for Josiah's human will, he surrendered. In his own words, Papa later said: "*Amazingly, God never abandoned me. This proved to me that God really loves me.*" [3]

Somewhere along the line of these experiences, Josiah felt inspired to go on a forty-day fast with intense praying. During the fast he had a final encounter with God which quickly propelled him into total and immediate compliance with God's will for his life. This was 1940 and Josiah was now 31 years of age. He related thus: "*...God with His mighty hand touched me heavily and* said, "whether you like it or not you will commence work in My vineyard this year." [4] How did God "touch" His servant? Josiah had a dream while sleeping out at his farmstead one day. In the dream, a certain old man came along and pinched him on his leg. By the time he woke up the leg had swollen and had a visible sore. Within two months Josiah became practically paralysed in that leg. While recollecting, Papa said: *"I just couldn't walk with the leg because the wound literally ate deep into my bones which became visible to the eye."* [5]

The sore soon became a really bad sight indeed to behold. Right now Josiah was no more complacent about God's pending call. He prayed with his whole heart that God would not abandon him at this point. Therefore when God's calling voice came again, the suffering man promptly responded: *"I will, Lord. Anywhere You send me, I will go."* [6] Thereafter God's instructions came clearly that Josiah was to leave home for Ile-Ife.

On the 10th of July 1940, Josiah Olufemi left Ondo and headed in the indicated direction. It was a 60km. journey from Ondo, but God told His man to go on foot, not minding the pain and sore on one of his legs. In tears and with pain in his heart Josiah complied with God's marching order without fail. Later in life Papa said that the trekking order was a punishment for his long staking out against God's call.

However on the long journey they had a sweet

fellowship-Father and son. God made Josiah to realise that He had sovereignly chosen him as His own servant, and it was not wise of him to have resisted for so long. Josiah in turn asked God for a clear evidence of God's call upon his life, and God gave him three key scriptures: Jeremiah 1:4-10; Isaiah 41:10-13; Romans 8:29-31. Though not lettered at all, but the first miracle of Josiah's life was that he was supernaturally enabled to open to those scripture passages in his Yoruba Bible and to read them. After this experience no one would open the holy Book to the illiterate man anymore because he could thenceforth open and read his (Yoruba) Bible by himself. He was also able to append his signature to documents rather than thumb print. Moreover one of the most notable gifts of the Spirit in Papa Akindayomi's life was the ability to hear the voice of God's Spirit so distinctly. It was phenomenal.

On his way to Ile-Ife, despite the discomfort of trekking for days, Josiah heard the voice of God saying repeatedly to him, *"Son I am going to use you."* The Ondo-Ife journey took several days through dense bush paths, but eventually the spiritual pilgrim arrived his destination.

ILE -IFE

Josiah Olufemi would be advancing in his tutelage in the things of God from this point on. After arriving Ile-Ife he had no idea where to turn next. In the midst of his contemplation a certain young boy showed up who wanted to know if he was looking for the *"Baba Aladura"* (of the C&S church) in that town. Josiah answered in the affirmative and subsequently followed the young boy. When they saw the Baba Aladura's house ahead the boy pointed the stranger to the house, and before Josiah could turn around to say *"thank you,"* behold he was all by himself. The boy had vanished into thin air! Stranger than fiction? Well, that was Josiah Olufemi's story as he related it to his wife. Could that have been an angel?

After meeting with the elderly *"Baba Aladura"* and telling his story, Josiah became part of the man's church located at Igbo-Itapa in Ile-Ife. While recounting the saga of his journey from Ondo to Ile-Ife before the Igbo-Itapa congregation Josiah told them how *"something sounding like an airplane"* hovered restlessly above his head as he travelled. Even though he couldn't see it with his eyes, but all through the journey *"the thing"* followed him. If he stopped somewhere to rest the *"airplane thing"* stopped also and kept hovering above his head. He could hear the humming sound audibly. As soon as he moved again *"the thing"* moved with him also. And so it was all the way night and day until he got to Ile-Ife.

What could *"the thing"* be? Who knows? Perhaps that was God's presence going with His servant to see him through the jungle and the bushes. No wonder Papa reported that he was never afraid nor scared of anything including wild animals on his journey, even though he had to sleep wherever nightfall met him. The Ile-Ife sojourn was most eventful and significant on many fronts for Josiah, including the fact that he never returned a bachelor as he had arrived there.

On Josiah's first day in church very interesting things began to happen-to him and to his host congregation. It was the usual 6:00 am early morning prayer *(ipade adura)*, and the little church was full, even though it was raining heavily. However there was a little anxiety in the congregation today. An *"elemi"* (seer/prophesier)lay prostrate on the floor in the full glare of the people. It was normal for *"elemis"* to go off in the spirit like that, but it didn't take long and they were out of it. Moreover they would keep making sounds *(sometimes coherent, sometimes not)*. But today this particular *"elemi"* had been gone a few hours and he neither moved hand nor leg. As a matter of fact no part of his body moved and he kept lying in that same position.

None present dared express their worst fears. The church elders prayed silently that the whole exercise today would not just turn awry. The concern within the congregation was palpable. Suddenly from the back there came a sharp voice announcing to the whole house that the man on the floor was indeed alive and not dead. The people should be calm and not fear. God had a special message for them through the *"elemi,"* whenever the man comes around they would receive the message.

Every eye turned in the direction of the voice, and lo and behold, it was the newcomer in their midst-Josiah Olufemi Akindolie. The Ondo man with the weird story and a bad sore on one of his legs. In the meanwhile Josiah stepped out into the pouring rain, stretched out his hands and commanded the downpour to cease.

Before long the heavy rain had reduced to a mere drizzle. That day's prayer meeting was suddenly turning out to be more exciting than the people had had it in a long time. Along with the new *"prophet"* in their midst, the people watched and waited until the *"elemi"* came round several hours later. That day's prayer meeting closed at 5:00 p.m., instead of the normal 7:00 a.m. Nobody left.

Within a very short space of time, Josiah Olufemi, despite his unsightly leg sore, had become the darling of the Igbo-Itapa congregation. He became very popular in the church, and they besieged him relentlessly. He began to be addressed as *"prophet"* and even his host, the *"Baba Aladura"* acknowledged God's grace upon Josiah's life; especially in the area of prayer. His prayers worked like *"magic."* The answers came almost instantly. It was at this church also that Josiah acquired his first prophet's handbell. The bell was said to have been purchased for him by the church leadership in obedience to God's directive.

FURTHER INSTRUCTIONS

A few days after Josiah's arrival God spoke again through some of the prophets in the church that Josiah was to go back home to Ondo and carry out some specific instructions. God said he should go and sell off all his personal belongings, and with the proceeds pay up any debts he might be owing anyone. He had been living as husband and wife with a woman to whom he was not married. He was to send her away. Finally his room in his father's house should be vacated and given up. He would never be returning there again to stay. *Whao!* One of the most heart-broken persons as a result of Josiah's action was his mother. Why leave home for good? Well, so says the Lord. And so Josiah departed his father's house permanently. Till Papa died in 1980 he never had cause to spend as much as two weeks in his native Ondo again. He was fully taken up with God's service and going only where God would send him.

On the 24th of July, 1940 Josiah left for Ondo in accordance with the Lord's bidding. Within five days he had gone and come back, having carried out all the given instructions. On his return to Ile-Ife God said to Josiah personally: **"You will not collect any salary throughout your life, for I the Lord shall be your Source and the Provider of your every need."** [7] Now Josiah became 100% God-dependent. But that was a promise God kept to the letter. It is an open secret that throughout his life and ministry Papa Akindayomi never took a salary in all his service for the Lord. He lived by faith all through.

MARRIAGE TO ESTHER EGBEDIRE

After returning to Ile-Ife young Prophet Josiah settled properly into the Igbo-Itapa church and became a very useful vessel unto the Lord and a great blessing unto the people. But God did not allow His servant to go unrewarded for his faithfulness and obedience either. The delectable Esther Egbedire, an Ife indegene and a member of the choir caught his attention.

The young lady was a ward to one of the elderly women of the church, whom she assists in making *eko* (cold pap). Esther's guardian was quite strict and never allowed the girl to be frivolous or wayward. God spoke to Prophet Josiah Olufemi that Esther was to be his wife. When Josiah was sure that God had put her love in his heart, he spoke to another elderly woman in the church who took the proposal to Esther's guardian.

However when Esther was intimated with the matter she got angry and took offence with all concerned. How dare those old women bring such wicked proposal to her? A poor prophet with nothing but a handbell, a funny dress and no income at all? It sounded like a cruel joke to the young woman. She was about 25. Having lost her father at a tender age, Esther's marriage dream had been to a comfortable man who at least would compensate for her early sufferings in life. How dare Prophet Josiah set his eye on her? It took a lot of persuasion and prayer and much counselling to pacify Esther.

Even a prominent prophet in Ile-Ife *(outside the Igbo-Itapa congregation)* had to be consulted over the matter. To re-assure her, the man was consulted in Esther's presence. They all knelt down to pray. Presently the man (Prophet Aaron) said to the reluctant bride-to-be: *"If you marry another person you will be miserable throughout your life. Even if you bear children for such a husband, the children will only make you miserable. But if you will ... marry this Prophet Josiah, He, the Lord will bless you and make you a blessing; because by marrying prophet*

Josiah God said He is sending you on a mission." [8]

Esther still did not like the idea, even though before Josiah's proposal, she herself claimed to have had a certain impression that Josiah would ask to be her husband. With time however she allowed God's Spirit to work on her and thus Esther Egbedire became Prophet Josiah's trophy from Ile-Ife in the year 1941. The young man was excused from paying any dowry on his young bride, and surprisingly Esther had no more objections. She even told Prophet Josiah later that she was happy to become a servant of God too like her husband. They eventually left Ile-Ife together. Church marriage proper was conducted when they arrived Lagos much later. On their arrival in Lagos they joined the C&S church (Oke Sioni) located somewhere on Ibadan Street at Ebute-Metta; and about 2 months later were joined in holy matrimony in this church.

IBADAN
Prophet Josiah left Ile-Ife gloriously and headed in the direction of Ibadan. His Ile-Ife experience had lasted a total of 6 months. It could not be ascertained how long he sojourned at Ibadan, but it was established that his brief Ibadan stay was also with an existing C&S church where he was as active and visible just as he had been at Ile-Ife. Before the end of 1941, the same year he left Ile-Ife Prophet Josiah headed for Lagos.

While at Ibadan, he had kept having the nudge that he was not yet where God wanted him. Where was it? He didn't know but he was sure it was not Ibadan. God kept telling him however that He was taking him somewhere. On the day the clear indication came that it was Lagos, Prophet Josiah promptly collapsed his tents again and was soon on his way, ably accompanied by his young and obedient wife, Esther Egbedire.

LAGOS SPELLS H-O-M-E!
MOSES ORIMOLADE TUNOLASE

Having been much used to the Cherubim and Seraphim set-up, Prophet Josiah Olufemi Akindole immediately identified himself with the church on his arrival in Lagos. Before the many sects and versions of the C&S prevalent today, the only C&S known worldwide was that founded in 1925 by Prophet Moses Orimolade Tunolase a.k.a "Baba Aladura."

The Oke Sioni place which became Prophet Josiah's home church was the first C&S congregation that Orimolade himself established when he started off his Movement in Lagos in 1925. Josiah was here until 1952 when they parted ways. While with this congregation, Prophet Josiah was much beloved by the presiding *"Baba Aladura,"* Prophet William Onanuga the man to whom Orimolade personally handed over. Orimolade *(the original "Baba Aladura")* had passed away in October, 1933, some eight years before Josiah's arrival in Lagos.

Onanuga particularly loved Josiah because he was zealous, passionate and a man of prayer, like the late C&S founder. According to Pastor J. A. O. Akindele,

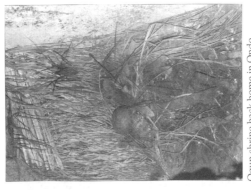

Ogun shrine back home in Ondo

Rev. Akindayomi's childhood home at Ondo (*now a Redeemed parish*)

Prophet Josiah Olufemi and Esther Egbedire

Papa with his faithful driver (*now Pastor*) Mulero

Papa on his way out with his Benz 280S

Papa's touring car, complete with carrier
and his signature sticker: JESUS IS CALLING YOU

Rev. Talabi,
Papa's
bossom friend

Winning smile,
Papa in quintesential
simple outfit

Pastor Timothy G. Oshokoya, (*aka "Brother T"*) First General Superintendent, Apostolic Faith, Nigeria

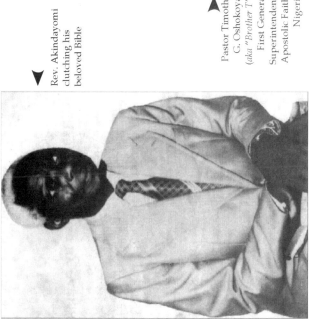

Rev. Akindayomi clutching his beloved Bible

W. F. Kumuyi,
General
Suprintendent,
Deeper Life
Bible Church

Rev. J. O. Akindayomi
in his famous
evangelist outfit,
complete with his
signature bowler hat

Papa in group photograph with first RCCG Youth Fellowship EXCO

The early crop of RCCG leadership, with Rev. J. O. Akindayomi, (*extreme left*) and Pastor Adeboye (*extreme right*)

Mama Akindayomi in deep reflection
over the journey of faith
(*picture taken shortly before her transition*)

Papa in later years, showing signs of fatigue

Papa's personal home at Ondo (*built post-humously in his name*)

Onanuga made Prophet Josiah the head of the C&S Prayer Band. From C&S history we discover that from inception its Prayer Band was the most formidable unit of the Movement. This Prayer Band *(perhaps due to its popularity)* broke away from the C&S Movement in 1930 under its leader, a certain Ezekiel A. Davies.

Perhaps the coming of Josiah with his prayer grace rekindled the C&S hope for the Prayer Band again. It is noteworthy that Papa Akindayomi also started his church as a prayer fellowship, called: **Ogo Oluwa Prayer Society.** Josiah lived, loved and breathed prayer!

The dynamic prophet was also a foremost evangelist who used to be sent on crusade assignments as far away as Kano in the Northern part of Nigeria. Before coming to Lagos to settle in early 1925, Orimolade had been an itinerant evangelist and had covered practically all the existing four Regions of Nigeria then. He was thus quite well known even in the northern parts of the country. On one of Prophet Josiah's crusade campaigns in Kano, a pregnant woman was raised by his prayers. She had died hours earlier of unknown causes. The dead woman was brought in while the crusade was going on and (evangelist) Prophet Josiah was notified. He readily came forth and prayed for the young woman who instantly came back to life. After this episode, Josiah himself also earned the title of *"Baba Aladura;"* as his fame continued to spread.

Even though the hand of the Lord was mightily evident

upon this young man but he hardly had any big vision for himself. His only passion was just to pray for people, see them delivered, healed and set free. It took others around him to see that he was destined for a greater future in God. While with the C&S Prophet Josiah was also a tremendous blessing to the church leadership. In the first place his presence in church any day meant more people would attend. And the church leadership liked that. In the second place when it was time to pray for the people, at least eighty per cent (80%) of people on the prayer queue wanted *"baba aladura"* Prophet Josiah to pray for them. Why? From experience and testimonies everyone knew that if the man prayed his prayers worked on the instant. You never had to come a second time over the same issue. It did not matter what the problem was: barrenness, complicated and complex cases of all kinds, demonic attacks, poison cases, unemployment etc.

Thus Prophet Josiah's time with the Cherubim and Seraphim was a time of tremendous blessing unto the people, and which they greatly appreciated. His two extra wives which eventually landed him in trouble with God came as gifts while with the C&S. Prophet Josiah was not even compelled to pay dowries for the wives because his benefactors wanted him to have them gratis. He did pay dowry for one though, his second wife Deborah.

Besides we hear that women used to throng the dynamic and handsome man of God literally throwing themselves at him, wanting at least a relationship. Many would tell him they were glad just to have his children, and that he didn't need to marry them. Apart from being ruggedly good-looking Prophet Josiah was also a six-footer.

However, like father Abraham, the quintessential spiritual pilgrim, for [this] Prophet Josiah also it was soon time again to say goodbye to his present company and move ahead to the next port of call as his God would indicate to him. But very many issues had to be sorted and settled first. He had been with the Lagos C&S for solid ten years.

Of course he went with his many wives.

NOTES

1)   Olusola, Ajayi (Dr.) DVM, Warrior of Righteousness:
     The Life and Ministry of Rev. J. O. Akindayomi
     (Abeokuta, Nigeria: Ordinance Publishing House, 1997), 18
2)   Ibid., 19
3)   Ibid., 19-20
4)   Ibid., 20
5)   Ibid., 20
6)   Ibid., 25
7)   Ibid., 29
8)   Ibid.,

CHAPTER TWO

"AND YE SHALL KNOW THE TRUTH..."

I T IS VERY INTERESTING TO NOTE THAT despite his many strange and rather uncommon experiences in things of the supernatural, Prophet Josiah had not yet had a definitive salvation experience. Even though it was clear to him now and settled in his heart that his destiny in life was to be a servant of God, full-time and that God meant to use him in great ways, but a number of things were yet unsettled.

Prophet Josiah already had an idea-via the several sovereign visitations and encounters that not only was God real, but He also talks to people and gives them Divine guidance, but he was yet to *know* the Lord.

This much he himself seemed to admit while reminiscing on one of his many actions at this period: *"Two years into my membership of the C&S, I'm sorry to say that I lost my salvation by committing the sin of adultery by which I took on another woman and I thus became a polygamist."* [1]

However, as the Lord had said: **"ye shall know the truth and the truth shall set you free"** (John 8:32), it reached a point of Prophet Josiah's involvement with the C&S when God began to raise personal issues with him and this began to create anxiety over his continued stay within that fold.

Like his Biblical namesake of old the young King Josiah, this Josiah was going to spearhead a major departure from the old pathways *(of the white garment church)* and his subsequent teachings and eventual pull-out were going to have far-reaching effects. As the history of the early Church reformers has revealed, right from John Wycliffe *(the first Bible translator*, 1330-1384); through men like John Huss (1372-1415); Martin Luther (1483-1546); John Calvin (1509-1564); John Knox (1514-1572); George Fox (1624-1691); the Wesley brothers, Catherine and William Booth of the Salvation Army and others; there's often this common thread: a passionate defence of the undiluted Word of God and the practice of the faith with the purity of the Spirit of Christ. As Roberts Liardon has observed in his Volume II of GOD'S GENERALS, history indeed is a blueprint of our past, and *"it tells a story that is always repeated somewhere else in time, some place in every generation,..."* [2]

Akindayomi was now going to chart a path for the church of the future, devoid of the rags of the past, and the Lord Jesus was going to lead him into it. In the words of Christian apologist and distinguished writer, C. S. Lewis: *"I do not think that all who choose wrong roads perish; but their rescue consists in being put back on the right road. A sum can be put right: but only by going back till you find the error and working it afresh from that point, never by simply going on."* [3]

Every reformer in Church history has always had not a personal vision of accomplishing this or that dream, but rather a vision of God Himself manifesting among His people. That vision is far superior to mere religion. Thus whenever such men raise their voice it is actually the voice of the Almighty thundering through an earthen vessel.

When Martin Luther faced an array of the European princes and lords at the now famous Diet of Worms confrontation in 1521, Emperor Charles V of Spain screamed at the reformer, *"Luther, the whole of Europe is against you."* With the fire of God burning in his heart and the flames shooting through his blazing eyes, the man of God shot back at the emperor, *"Emperor, Luther is against the whole of Europe!"* Why? God had revealed to His man that **"the just shall live by faith"** but the Roman Catholic Church powers insisted that people could only be saved through works, especially as prescribed by the Church laws. And some of the prescriptions were as ridiculous as that visiting holy sites at Rome and viewing certain artifacts from the past would lead to forgiveness of a person's sins.

Thus Rome became the place to go (a Mecca) if someone wanted to really stockpile goodness into his account with the church, (but not with God). So where's the place of the cross of Christ where sin was judged, and the power of the blood shed to atone for the sinner's life? The Catholic authority said everything resided in Rome. By Divine revelation Luther thought otherwise now, even though he had been a part of this system for most of his life.

Rev. Akindayomi after God began to point things out to him tried to stay back and begin to effect corrections from within the C&S, but he discovered that the system was too set in its ways and inflexible for that. He started by initiating an independent Bible Study away from the church while maintaining his membership with the C&S: He explains his action thus: *"For the fact that I was quite opposed to many of the Seraphim church practices, God again inspired me to gather the youth for group Bible Study. At this time we used to meet and study in the home of one man named Adedoyin, living on Ondo street. This Bible study started in 1946. The main reason for starting this Bible study was that I did not want to leave the Seraphim church, and moreover I felt that if we taught the younger people the knowledge of the Word of God and they had deep knowledge it could prove a challenge to the older people, who also could show interest in Bible knowledge."* [4] But things refused to work out that simply and so a separation eventually became inevitable.

According to history, the (church) canon law was the

same as the 'commandments of God' to the faithful Roman Catholic. But really it was all a game. A ruse. It took Luther's fury under God, having gone the whole hog and never encountering God's forgiveness nor the reality of His existence; to dismantle the mountain of errors. Luther painstakingly searched the Scriptures over a four-year period of diligent study. Where was true authority, and who had it-the Pope or the Lord?

When Luther eventually saw the light, all the clout and powers of the Papal machinery could not hold him down. The fight was long-drawn and bitter but the truth prevailed.

Martin Luther himself later in life, explained the source of the strength and energy to successfully confront such a formidable entity as the Roman Catholic hierarchy: *"It is not our work ...for man alone could not begin to carry such a thing. It is another who is driving the wheel, one whom the papists do not see; therefore they put the blame on us."* [5]

In the book of Hebrews the apostle Paul gave a Biblical foundation and understanding of Reformation thus:

"The Holy Ghost this signifying, that the way into the holiest of all was not yet made manifest, while as the first tabernacle was yet standing: Which was a figure for the time then present, in which were offered both gifts and sacrifices, that could not make him that did the service perfect, as pertaining to the conscience; Which stood only in meats and drinks, divers washings, and carnal ordinances, imposed on them

until the time of reformation" (Hebrews 9: 8-10).

So you see, there will always be that which fills a gap and only serves to prepare the way into the holiest of all. These things subsist until the time of Reformation. When the Reformation wind begins to blow it's like a hurricane, pulling down and carrying away every obstruction on its way. And the destination is always God-never this or that emphasis of ministry or church doctrine. Apostle Peter says the end or ultimate purpose of (our) faith is the salvation of our souls. Thus we should be ever ready and prepared to face fiery trials, defending the faith until **"the appearing of Jesus Christ"** (See I Peter 1: 7). Until the reformer gets to God and touches Him, he does not stop. This is always why nothing is too sacred to discard or dispose and no company too precious to separate from, the moment God indicates a departure from them to His man on the spot.

In light of the above one could then begin to understand why Prophet Josiah at this time seemed so hard on himself and quite unsparing of everyone and everything around him- a Higher Power was dictating his every action and move, and also granting him the strength of spirit to obey.

In the Bible when young King Josiah seemed to suddenly stumble upon the Book of the Law and had the contents read to him, Judah immediately became a target of Reformation. Josiah's subsequent actions had serious ripples effects upon the entire land of Judah. After causing the same Book to be read to the people, Josiah began to walk with the Lord by covenants and pledged his people to the same lifestyle (see 2 Kings 22:10-13; 23:1-28). Among the notable actions taken by King Josiah was the destruction of idolatry in the land: "Moreover the workers with familiar spirits, and the wizards, and the images, and the idols, and all the abominations that were spied in the land of Judah and in Jerusalem, did Josiah put away, that he might perform the words of the law which were written in the book..." (2 Kings 23: 24).

In Luther's time the place to go was neither Jerusalem nor Judah but Rome. People were mandated to visit Rome and to view all kinds of relics, images and artifacts. These included what was claimed to be the silver coins that Judas received for betraying Jesus and a sampling of the milk from the virgin Mary's breast! There was also the Scala Sancta, Pontius Pilate's staircase where Jesus stood to be judged by the crowd before His crucifixion. And as for this staircase a person couldn't just look at them; he had to climb them reverently saying a specific prayer for each of the twenty-eight steps.

The Catholic system told the people that one trip up the stairs had enough power in it to release a dead relative from purgatory. Among the most notorious extra-scriptural doctrines of the Catholic Church for which Luther started his confrontation was that of purgatory. According to the Catholic church, purgatory was a kind of a halfway-house between heaven and hell. It was for people not good enough to enter heaven yet not bad enough to go to hell. So God kept them in purgatory expecting their living relatives to make up for their required measure of goodness by doing good works, calculated only in silver coins (money).

History records that the Pope's man on duty for the sale of indulgences to obtain release from purgatory was a priest named John Tetzel. Tetzel's popular phrase while auctioning his ware was thus: *"As soon as the coin in the coffers rings, the soul from purgatory springs."* [6] As a result people battling with personal guilt and fear poured money into a system that took them no nearer God than the system itself was. Rome was also supposed to be the burial place of both Paul and Peter's bodies. One church in Rome was said to have even claimed to be in possession of the twelve-foot beam on which Judas hanged himself! People were subtly pummelled into visiting all these worthless sites and offering countless kinds of ineffectual prayer. Luther came along and threw a strong spanner in the works. But it was God's doing. The torch he ignited eventually lighted the whole world.

As God began to deal with Prophet Josiah over issues the man realised that a long battle for truth was ahead.

Yes, the man could pray with signs and wonders following, he could display all kinds of power gifts, but his own personal life had never been addressed by the Lord. God needed to do this so that the man could be fit spiritually as God's battle axe. Father Abraham had walked with God for very many years. He had fallen and risen several times while his real potentials in God just hung somewhere up there. However when God was ready to launch His man into the reality of his calling, He said to him: *"walk before me, and be thou perfect"* (Gen. 17: 1b). It was time now to cut covenant, and by implication demands would begin to be made; because God would be checking and inspecting everything. The journey into the depths of the spirit begins now.

PREPARING THE NEW WINESKIN
Back at the C&S presiding Prophet Onanuga particularly valued Prophet Josiah so much because he was a tremendous blessing to the congregation, and a great asset to the C&S organisation as a whole. A level of liberty was granted him to operate freely within the system.

Prophet Josiah himself appreciated this affection and liberty so much that even when God's dealings with him got to the point of urgency he was somewhat unwilling to depart his C&S home. He was cognisant of the fact that the two times he had been anointed and consecrated for the Lord's work were at the C&S- first with the Igbo-Itapa congregation at Ile-Ife, and with the Oke Sioni congregation in Lagos. He also did not forget that the Lord had given him his first wife from among the C&S. Quite a basket of debt, but something else within was disturbing the prophet about his C&S roots.

This brewing new wine tried to stay back inside the old wineskin, but neither could contain the other. Having tried and failed in 1946, he tried again in 1949: *"In 1949 I gathered people in the church in the hope that they would yield to the gospel, but nevertheless that proved impossible. Rather than change, they were just telling the same old stories. The Spirit within me that was earnestly seeking the truth of God's Word kept urging me to go ahead. This made me to depart from there in 1952."* [7]

Somehow his C&S brethren did not share Prophet Josiah's passion and burden: *"After a lot of labour and effort for the Bible study, and I saw that there was no headway, and that the people did not want to accept the teachings of the Bible, I resolved to be going to the water front for prayers."* [8]

By 1947 the flow of people resorting to him at the water front and needing his prayer ministry and prophetic guidance had become quite high and more space was needed. Besides he himself said that a lot of 'big people' started coming to see him there. This was what he did next: *"After this we removed the prayer meeting from the water front and we started meeting in my house. At this time I was living at 34, Oloto Street, Ebute-Metta, Lagos"* [9] (Memoirs). Even though still a bona-fide C&S member, but the openness of the waterfront had made Prophet Josiah semi-independent and he now had a growing independent following. Papa himself said: *"Right now the number of people coming for the prayer meeting began to increase and they were coming from all kinds of churches."* [10]

Initially when he had started the daily prayer meeting back in 1947, certain disgruntled elements within the church hierarchy had complained to Prophet Onanuga that Prophet Josiah was *"doing his own thing"* despite being a C&S ordained prophet. Actually the complainants' real pain was that their colleague was getting all the attention because of the operation of the gifts of the Spirit in his life. Much against their expectations however, Onanuga never once rebuked nor stopped Prophet Josiah from his ministry efforts. He used to tell the dissemblers that no doubt God had called the younger man and he should be allowed to do the work. Moreover it is reported that Prophet Josiah being a very forthright and wise person, Onanuga found him an invaluable help in troubled times within the length and breath of the C&S organisation. Prophet Josiah was so good at conflict resolution that he was always the leadership's ambassador of peace in all the C&S Districts. Therefore Onanuga was not willing to entertain frivolous reports about this useful vessel.

However, soon Prophet Onanuga died, and somehow the liberty Josiah had freely enjoyed stood in jeopardy. After Onanuga, a certain Prophet Amodu *(a converted Moslem)* took over mantle of leadership of the Oke Sioni congregation and by implication, the C&S Movement.

As soon as Amodu came in the attackers went to work again, but somehow they couldn't secure Amodu's co-operation either. Even when insinuations were made that Prophet Josiah was probably gathering people for the so-called Bible Study because he wanted to split the Orimolade C&S and start his own Movement; Amodu told the agitators to leave Josiah alone. As far as he was concerned he saw nothing wrong in Prophet Josiah teaching people the Bible.

Like the late Onanuga, Amodu was also quite elderly before joining the C&S and finding himself in leadership position. So Josiah's dynamism was a great asset to him. Thus Prophet Josiah continued his home based Bible study group but trouble showed up soon afterwards.

Since God had supernaturally enabled him to read his (Yoruba) Bible on his way to Ile-Ife, Papa had formed the habit of studying his Bible during his prayer time. Later in his ministry, even professors and Bible scholars could not match his insight and revelation into the Word of God, because Papa depended 100% upon the Holy Spirit, realising his own limitations as an uneducated person.

THE RULE OF LAW
While quenching his own desperate thirst for the truth, Prophet Josiah was also feeding his faithful 'regulars' at the Bible Study. Soon he began to notice very disturbing discrepancies between certain practices within the C&S Movement and the Word of God. For Prophet Josiah therefore this period (between 1947-51) became years of serious soul searching and spiritual auditing. He couldn't account for many of his own personal practices when

placed alongside the revealed Word of God. For instance he could find no biblical support for polygamy, which he was involved in among others.

Then there was this practice of going to the cemetery to "pray" and make things happen; apart from other fetish practices he had never really personally agreed with. His exposure to God's Word began to establish some of his doubts and misgiving.

Actually the practice of necromancy (see Deuteronomy 18:10-12) crept into the C&S soon after the demise of its founder, Prophet Moses Orimolade Tunolase, who died in 1933. The resultant succession struggles led to certain of the church prophets visiting the founder's burial site in order to determine who should occupy what positions, and sometimes to settle quarrels and grievances. This trend soon became a norm. Prophet Josiah came to meet this practice in the C&S, but chose not to join the extra-Biblical train, and surely that stand did not endear him to certain powers that be within the system. Moreover when Onanuga too died, the Oke Sioni prophets also began frequenting Orimolade's burial site for "consultations." Even though not agreeing with them, Josiah had strong words of caution and warning for his colleagues. None listened to him.

In the meanwhile his home crowd steadily increased. Papa used to conduct them on a forty-day prayer retreat at the water front during lent after which he encourages the people to return to their various churches. By May

1951 the group moved again to S. A. Olonade's residence at 9, Willoughby street, and Prophet Josiah gave it the name **"Ogo Oluwa" (Glory of God) Prayer Society.** Prayers and Bible Study continued regularly.

It soon became very clear that Prophet Josiah Olufemi Akindolie (later Akindayomi) would never blend in with the prevailing leadership and practices in the C&S. In the words of C. S. Lewis: *"Good as it ripens, becomes continually more different not only from evil but from other good."* [11] Prophet Josiah was maturing spiritually and thus could no longer continue with the C&S style, but neither would he be quiet about the areas of contradiction to God's Word. However the hierarchy would have none of that. Therefore towards the end of 1952, seeing that the man would leave anyway, the C&S excommunicated the *"errant"* prophet. He was accused (among other things) of *"anti-church"* activities such as organising Bible Study outside the C&S ambience, with the motive of sheep stealing. With this development, Prophet Josiah gracefully exited the C&S church finally and permanently before the close of 1952.

According to the famous Prince of Preachers, Charles Spurgeon (1834-1892), *"Fellowship with known and vital error is participation in sin."* [12] And with that declaration Spurgeon withdrew from the Baptist Union (in 1887). One of the controversial cardinal doctrinal Statements of the Baptist Union was that the days of miracles ended with the Apostles of the Lamb. Obviously Spurgeon must have disagreed with that! On his way out he left the following words behind for his Baptist brethren: *"I am quite sure that the best way to promote Union is to promote truth. It would not do for us to be all united together by yielding to one another's mistake"* [13]

Like Spurgeon, Prophet Josiah separated from his roots on principle.

RE-ALIGNMENTS

Having now renounced his membership of the C&S Movement, Prophet Josiah began to thirst for a deeper understanding of the things of God. During this critical period he was privileged to sit under the ministry of Rev. Odunaike, the then General Overseer of the Foursquare Gospel Church in Nigeria and subsequently gave his life to Christ publicly in a definite salvation experience. Now Prophet Josiah was born again! For this new man old things had passed away and behold all things are become brand new. His every step now would be subject strictly to the scrutiny of the Word of God. At this time also Papa sought outside help in a bid to transform his group into a thoroughly evangelical one: *"In 1952, a man named Thompson used to come to help us with Bible study. Moreover brother Odunaike used to come to teach us gospel choruses. Brother Osiyemi was the one who helped us with training on evangelism, which now made us to become completely evangelical"* [14]

Soon afterwards the habit of burning candles and incense for prayers was stopped, based on what Papa discovered in Scriptures that a burning candle (lamp) referred either to the Spirit of God or the Spirit-quickened human spirit (Psalms 18: 28; Proverbs 20: 27). It is never a physical candle, and actually answer to prayer had nothing to do with a lighted candle. Secondly on the use of incense the Bible reveals that it is the prayers of God's saints that are as incense ascending unto His throne (Revelation 8: 3-4). It is nothing to do with physical burning of incense(s). Thus Prophet Josiah stopped the practice.

Next the "white garment" was set aside. Prophet Josiah found out from the book of Revelation that the "white robe" in reference was actually the righteousness of the saints of God whose hearts have been washed clean in the blood of the Lamb-Jesus Christ, and not a physical white dress which very many times is covering up all kinds of ungodliness and iniquity.

Soon Papa also dropped the title 'prophet' and began to answer to 'Reverend.' For him, his greatest desire now was to know the true and living God in all His holiness and righteousness; and to serve Him with all his heart, soul and spirit. These moves were not popular ones at all because the man had no human guide or sample for his actions, only the leading of the Holy Spirit. And to the best of his ability Prophet Josiah was also determined to follow anything he discovered in the holy Scriptures. However to onlookers, especially his former associates back at the C&S, this Prophet Josiah of a fellow must have lost his senses. Really? Time would tell.

PAINFUL PARTINGS

After his salvation experience, the budding man of God found himself now on a level playing ground, especially as regards certain knotty issues of his own personal life that God had been dealing with him about while still on the other side. Besides he began to thirst earnestly for the experience of sanctification as well, and he discovered that this required that he came clean with God all-round. In his days at the Aladura church, Papa had inadvertently acquired two extra wives apart from Esther Egbedire his first wife and with whom he had had a church wedding. The Lord told him he would have to sort himself out in that area before they could proceed further together on this unique journey. It was hard, very hard, because at least one of his two other wives already had a number of children for him, besides he had paid dowry on this one and met her father to formally ask her hand in (traditional) marriage. But now God must be obeyed.

Barely two months after their excommunication from C&S Rev. Josiah Olufemi Akindolie stood before his little band of followers one day and blurted out: *"God spoke to me that I am the number one adulterer in this place."* [15] What? What is the man talking about? Who is an adulterer? What's the definition of adultery? The man of God understood what agitations must be going on in the hearts of his people. They all came from different church backgrounds, and many out of the C&S with him. Among them were men like him with three or four wives, and some of the wives were even now faithful members of the new fellowship already. Some of the men threatened to go back to the C&S, and a particular man was said to have actually left, because his own second wife became born again and chose to restitute her ways before the Lord.

Having done everything to stop this much beloved second wife from leaving and failing to secure Rev. Josiah's intervention in the matter, the man angrily left the Ogo Oluwa Prayer Society back to the C&S. But he stayed only two months and returned under Rev. Josiah's leadership. This step encouraged more women to restitute their own ways too, under no pressure from anyone. Papa patiently explained to his people in the following words: *"All of us are learning from the Bible together. As each person observes his or her way as unrighteous he or she must be free to restitute."* [16]

Some other men who went back to the C&S as a result of this issue never returned, but Rev. J. O. Akindolie still went ahead to do what the Lord had told him to do. One of the restitutions Papa did also was to go before his former C&S brethren to apologise that whenever candles were requested from prayer seekers, since only one or two was often required for the said prayer the leftovers were often appropriated by the prophets. Papa asked to be forgiven for the times he had taken such candles home for personal use. Word started to go around that Prophet Josiah was "confessing," i.e. in the style of those accused of witchcraft or other diabolical practices those days.

Despite reproaches like this one, the man of God went ahead with actions that proved his convictions.

On the marriage issue Papa told his own people that God's instruction to him was that His arrangement for man was one man, one wife regardless of how men had twisted the issue. Therefore only his first wife was permitted for him before God, the others were extras and should be let go. Before now his third wife, popularly called *Sisi Mi*, a very tough and contentious woman, whom he married in 1949, had already left as a result of some misunderstanding. *Sisi Mi* was recalled for a final settlement and because he wanted peace at all cost, Papa gave her permission to take whatever she wanted from the house before leaving. Sisi Mi had no child for Papa.

As early as possible that morning Papa had sent Mama Egbedire out so that she would not be involved in any way. Papa himself left afterwards so that Sisi Mi could feel free. By the time Papa and Mama came back home later that day, they had hardly a mattress to sleep on nor pot to cook with! Sisi Mi had swept the house clean. But Papa did not mind the losses.

Consider the following observation: *"You cannot take all luggage with you on all journeys; on one journey even your right hand and your right eye may be among the things you have to leave behind. We are not living in a world where all roads are radii of a circle and where all, if followed long enough, will therefore draw gradually nearer and finally meet at the centre: rather in a world where every road, after a few miles, forks into two, and each of those into two again, and at each fork you must make a decision."* [17]

Rev. Josiah Olufemi Akindolie arrived this crucial cross-roads and make that decision indeed did he. God had spoken, who will not but hear? Thus on a very painful, costly, but obedient note Papa gave notice of his intentions to his second wife, Deborah.

THE ENTRANCE OF DEBORAH

Prophet Josiah's marriage to Deborah took place in 1943, two years into his first wife's four-year barrenness experience. Right now his marriage to Deborah was well over eight years and children had become involved. What to do? Hard, painful, difficult and costly as the action was going to be, Prophet Josiah chose to obey the Lord. On that note he decided to discuss the terms of disengagement with his heartbroken second wife.

Recalling that traumatic episode, Madam Deborah, now 84 and a Mother-in-Israel with the C&S, had this to say: *"When Woli (i.e Prophet) without any quarrel a sked me to go because of what he said his God was telling him, and all my pleadings did not change his mind, yet I really loved him, I decided to take him to court. He did not contest it, so the court asked me to return the £12:6s he had paid as my dowry back to him. Woli did not take the money but said I should keep it to take care of our little son with me at the time of this separation. But I tell you I can never forget Akindayomi. He was a very handsome man, a faithful lover and a very impeccable man. He's a good man. I know we shall meet again!"* [18]

It was a very difficult last day with Deborah, this beloved second wife, whom he had married just two years after his arrival in Lagos, when things were so hard for him and his first wife.

Don't forget that for the first four years of their arrival in Lagos, Prophet Josiah and his first wife Esther Egbedire had no child. It was a very difficult period for the young, struggling couple. Papa Akindayomi captured the mood of that period in the following words: "*My wife was barren for complete four years. She did not once become pregnant... I was still at this time being wonderfully used for the Lord's work. Some women who had no children for about 20 years came to me and I prayed for them and the Lord would answer, but my own wife remained barren.*" [19]

In the midst of this difficulty he took on a second wife. Eight years down the line the Lord brings forth His surgical knife to separate His servant from some of the errors of his past. Rev. Josiah was most sorry and apologetic for the turn of events, and pledged to retain and train the children accruing from their relationship but Deborah herself had to go. Rev. Josiah also told Deborah that in the event she chooses to remain unmarried he would take care of her all his days. But should she decide otherwise he released her from his heart, and therefore she was free to be married to any other man of her choice. Afterwards, he prayed for her and assured her that God was going with her and would give her peace and blessing wherever else she went. Of course Deborah was well married again later with children. When Papa died she and her second husband came around to celebrate his home going.

From this point on Prophet Josiah's household became monogamous. Soon he changed his names from Josiah Olufemi Ogunribido Akindolie *(originally changed from Ogundolie)* to Josiah Olufemi Akindayomi. Akindayomi being his grandfather's first name which his own father too had earlier adopted. And so the Reformation train moved ahead.

GROWTH OF OGO-OLUWA PRAYER SOCIETY

Old habits, they say, die hard. Even though no more with the C&S Papa continued the practise of going to pray at the waterfront. No matter the situation with him, one thing Papa could not neglect to do was pray; and the lagoon front was a favourite for him. He loved and enjoyed prayer. Even though he was no more with the C&S, but people already knew him. Therefore as messy and quite unpleasant as the lagoon front was then, crowds of people resorted to Baba Aladura there just to have him pray for them. They used to refer to him as *"Baba to n riran,"* (i.e. the man that sees visions).

With Papa as the head, there were twelve other men committed as founding members of the Ogo Oluwa Prayer Society in the year 1952. Among these were Bro. S. A. Olonade who eventually became Church Secretary. Reports have it that Olonade it was who assisted Rev. Akindayomi in translating the name *"Ijo Irapada ti Olorun"* to Redeemed Christian Church of

God. Members eventually came variously from the CMS (Anglican Communion), Cherubim & Seraphim Prayer Band, United Native African Church, Methodist Church, while others were either Moslem or pagan converts. A formal setting was evolving. In-depth Bible Study preceded the intense prayer sessions. Bible Study was on Tuesdays with ample opportunity for questions and answers. Subsequently Sunday service was added. The organised group continued its meetings at No. 9,Willoughby Street, before moving finally to 1, Cemetery Street, both at Ebute Metta. This place till today serves as the headquarters parish of the RCCG.

With the expansion of the work and more exposure, Papa later changed the name of his fellowship from Ogo Oluwa to **"Apostolic Church of Africa."** Trouble soon came with the use of that name.

The Apostolic Faith church, Nigeria with its international headquarters at Portland, Oregon in the United States had been around awhile before Rev. Akindayomi started his own church down the road in 1952. Through the concerted efforts of Timothy G. Oshokoya, who eventually became its first Superintendent General, the Apostolic Faith fully registered its presence in Nigeria by 1942. Their first mission and headquarters was located at Moloney Street, off Cemetery Street in Ebute-Metta just a stone throw from where Rev. Akindayomi came to station his own church.

In the year 1939 Oshokoya had come in contact with an Apostolic Faith material, the reading of which subsequently led to his conversion. So stirred and challenged was the man that he decided to write Portland, Oregon for more Gospel materials, and they regularly obliged him. Along with his four prayer partners then, Oshokoya faithfully distributed the reading materials around. Subjects addressed included salvation, sanctification, Holy Spirit baptism, etc. By the time the Apostolic Faith mission was well established in Nigeria they would be receiving large consignments of tracts for distribution to other churches and groups for evangelistic campaigns. When churches or groups received such tracts, they stamped the back with their own names and address(es)before distribution during outdoor preaching engagements.

Rev. Akindayomi's group also used to receive the tracts from Apostolic Faith and use same for evangelism. But somewhere along the line Papa decided to change his own group's name to Apostolic Church of Africa. Why the name change?

Sometime around 1954 Rev. Akindayomi's Ogo Oluwa Society came in contact with the Apostolic Faith Mission of South Africa, a ministry founded in 1910 in South Africa by Dr. John G. Lake (1870-1935) , with headquarters in Johannesburg. With hopes of a partnership on both sides, the Apostolic Faith Mission of South Africa sent one of its missionaries, a certain Mr. Billingham to Nigeria in 1955 to explore the possibilities of a merger. By 1956 an agreement was indeed reached after several months of discussion, and this was when Rev. Akindayomi's church assumed the name: **Apostolic Faith Mission of (South) Africa (Nigeria Branch)**.[20] Papa recorded that a friend of his, Mr. Oshunkeye that introduced him to G. Lake's ministry: *"...my friend, Mr. Oshunkeye had been writing to some white people in South Africa. ...these white people wrote to my friend Oshunkeye that they wanted to visit Nigeria. After my friend received this letter he came to my place and said we should go and receive them at the airport. ... we conferred together on matters of the gospel. After much deliberation over possibilities of collaboration between their church and ours, they agreed that we should join up with them, and we signed an agreement. After the signed agreement we also agreed to change our church name to Apostolic Faith Mission of South Africa."* [21]

However, the Apostolic Faith neighbours of Rev. Akindayomi took exception to the new name when it came to their notice, because to them, Apostolic was their "name." Thus an Apostolic Faith tract that Papa had had translated from English into Yoruba and stamped with the new name of **"Apostolic Church of (South) Africa"** didn't go down well with the Apostolic Faith (Nigeria) church at all. The story had it that they called for Rev. Akindayomi to answer their query and submit the whole consignment of tracts, which he promptly did. Papa's group had been using the tracts for their regular evangelism/preaching outings. But when the tracts got to Apostolic Faith headquarters the whole lot was set ablaze!

Papa did not take kindly to this action at all. He was not
happy that the money expended on the Gospel materials
had been wasted, and secondly that the Body of Christ
was being divided on petty issues as nomenclature. If
Apostolic Faith wouldn't permit him to use the tracts, at
least they could make use of them. Why burn them up?
He was upset.

Particularly Papa was very bitter in his heart with
Brother T. *(popular appellation for Pastor Timothy G.
Oshokoya).* One of the struggles of Rev. Akindayomi's
life which apparently these more "comfortable"
Apostolic Faith leaders did not know was that his little
church was a complete work of faith. They had no
foreign affiliation nor support. His hard-line stance on
restitution, repentance, holiness, etc did not afford him
a large or "rich" congregation, besides he would not
receive just any kind of offering into the work.

Thus at this foundation stage most financial obligations
for church work fell directly on Papa's head, which
necessitated him many times to sell off some of his
meagre personal belongings in order to raise money. He
was deeply pained to the heart therefore to see such
precious and costly investment being set ablaze right
before his eyes. It was an injury he wasn't planning to
forget. But for God's mercy this *"little"* offence would
have cost the man of God his eternity.

Interestingly by 1960 the relationship with the Apostolic Faith Mission of South Africa came to an end: *"Up until this time our church had not been registered with the Federal Government of Nigeria. By the efforts and labours of these white people our church became registered with the government. A while after we had joined up with the South African church, Nigerian government said it was severing all relations with South Africa and decreed that no one should write to nor receive letters from South Africa. This issue resulted in us stopping to write to them, and which led to the end of our collaboration. But for that decree we wouldn't have ceased to work with the people."* [22]

Consequent upon the above Rev. Akindayomi's group slightly amended its own nomenclature and became: **the Apostolic Faith Mission of West Africa**,[23] to reflect the current position of things.

With time Papa eventually received the name Redeemed Christian Church of God in a vision: *"In 1956 I went to Oshogbo. While I was praying God spoke to me and He showed me that* **"Redeemed Christian Church of God"** *shall be the name of this church. From Oshogbo I wrote a letter to Brother S. A. Olonade concerning what God told me about this change of name. From that time till today we have been answering to the name that God Himself personally gave to this church."* [24]

And this was how the name RCCG came to be. The teething period of the Ogo Oluwa fellowship had given way to considerable stability and strength. The official birth date of the Redeemed Christian Church of God however stands as 1952.

R. C. C. G: THE LITTLE FLOCK OF GOD
The Redeemed Christian Church of God eventually found a home at No. 1, Cemetery Street, (now 1-5 Redemption Street) , Ebute Metta in the heart of Lagos. It had taken ten years of sweat and labour, transiting from the Cherubim & Seraphim to get to this point.

The whole set-up was a dingy all-planks affair built by communal effort. As a matter of fact the waterfront had to be reclaimed with much sand filling and prayer, but it was a happy band of people under the able leadership of the tall Ondo man who could pray anything out of heaven. They finished the work and soon settled down to the serious business of fellowship and growth.

NOTES
1) This is My Story: An authentic posthumous Autobiography of Rev. Josiah O. Akindayomi (One-Hour Books, USA, 2010), 145
2) Roberts Liardon, God's Generals II: The Roaring Reformers (New Kensington, PA 15068: Whitaker House, 2003), ii
3) C. S. Lewis, The Great Divorce. (New York, NY: Harper Collins, 2001), viii
4) This is My Story: An authentic posthumous Autobiography of Rev. Josiah O. Akindayomi (One-Hour Books, USA, 2010), 155
5) Roberts Liardon, God's Generals II: The Roaring Reformers (New Kensington, PA 15068: Whitaker House, 2003), 151
6) Ibid., p.140
7) This is My Story: An authentic posthumous Autobiography of Rev. Josiah O. Akindayomi (One-Hour Books, USA, 2010), 155
8) Ibid., p. 155
9) Ibid., p. 155-156
10) Ibid., p.156
11) C. S. Lewis, The Great Divorce. (New York, NY: Harper Collins, 2001), viii
12) "Charles Spurgeon: Becoming a Man or Woman of the Word," Life Magazine (Lagos, Nigeria: Life Press Ltd. 2004), 14

14) This is My Story: An authentic posthumous Autobiography of Rev. Josiah O. Akindayomi (One-Hour Books, USA, 2010), 159

15) Olusola, Ajayi (Dr.) DVM, **Warrior of Righteousness:** The Life and Ministry of Rev. J. O. Akindayomi (Abeokuta, Nigeria: Ordinance Publishing House, 1997), 49

17) C. S. Lewis, The Great Divorce, (New York, NY: Harper Collins, 2001),viii

18) Author's interview with Madam Deborah at her home (2007).

19) This is My Story: An authentic posthumous Autobiography of Rev. Josiah O. Akindayomi (One-Hour Books, USA, 2010), 144

20) Ayodeji Abodunde, **A Heritage of Faith: an History of Christianity in Nigeria**, (Ibadan, Nigeria: Pierce Watershed Media Company, 2009), 408.

21) This is My Story: An authentic posthumous Autobiography of Rev. Josiah O. Akindayomi (One-Hour Books, USA, 2010), 159

22) Ibid., p. 160

24) Ayodeji Abodunde, **A Heritage of Faith: an History of Christianity in Nigeria**, (Ibadan, Nigeria: Pierce Watershed Media Company, 2009),408

25) This is My Story: An authentic posthumous Autobiography of Rev. Josiah O. Akindayomi (One-Hour Books, USA, 2010), 160

CHAPTER THREE

THE SOUND
AND THE FURY

YEARS OF ESTABLISHMENT

WHEN THE NAME REDEEMED CHRISTIAN Church of God was revealed to Rev. Akindayomi, it came with a mandate from the Almighty God that the church should go to the ends of the earth. God had clearly commanded His servant, *"Prepare a people for the Lord."* The man of God took that command to heart and set his mind squarely on fulfilling the mandate. It was a determination that cost blood and sweat.

THE "EARLY" CHURCH

In the style of the early apostles in the Acts, Papa raised his church as the baby of his womb which must be nurtured with much prayer and watchfulness. No member was left in doubt whether Papa was a loving father or not, but they all knew too that his own love did not spell "soft." Not at all!

Any day you got carried away and found yourself on the wrong side of Papa you got a full dose of his other side head on. Doctrines were strict and closely monitored. Women could not come to church without their head scarves on. No hats were allowed. Their dresses and skirts had to be at a certain length and could have no slits at the back. If a female member tried to contravene the laid down dress code she was promptly sent back home!

Women could not treat their hair nor wear make-up. If you belonged in Papa's church as a single woman, men were not permitted to talk to you on the road, much less visit you at home. Papa's biological daughters particularly were personally monitored by him. Any day either of his two daughters in the choir mistakenly dosed during the sermon, like a crack of the whip they would suddenly hear, "*Duro, st and up!*" Or "*Bunmi, stand up!*" The offender might remain like that for the rest of the message. Whenever they were returning from choir practice at night, Papa had a way of suddenly springing up behind them or sometimes waiting for them at home to give them a full account of how many men greeted them before they got home. As a result, the girls were quite wary of any form of untoward conduct.

Church members generally must not be friends with unbelievers, it didn't matter who they were. If you befriended unbelievers, Papa made you realise that you must be a sinner too. Thus there was a close communal spirit in the little church. Everyone belonged to the other.

A new convert was not taken into the fold immediately. Thus converts' follow-up was rather vigorous. Papa wanted to confirm the veracity of a conversion if it was genuine or not. Therefore when a prospective convert was brought to church, Papa preached the salvation message personally to them all over again. No matter what subject Papa preached on, he must come back to the salvation message. He did not care how many times a person had heard it, he preached salvation until he was convinced the person was saved. And each time Papa preached on salvation and you felt convicted over an issue, you were required to come to the front to declare your readiness to follow the Lord at whatever cost. Coming to the front to repent wasn't a once for all affair.

When a convert's stand has been firmly established, he is then sent to the Salvation Foundation class, where he will also receive lessons for Water Baptism by immersion. After successfully going through these processes, exams were conducted. If you passed all your exams then you were graduated into the church proper. You become a recognised member of the church. Anyone that fails here could not give offerings, do any work in the church or do anything for the church.

CHURCH WORKERS

Workers' meeting was instituted by Papa and it commenced from 6:00 a.m. A serious church worker could not come one minute behind that time. Papa was a strict disciplinarian. He used to tell his church in Yoruba, *"Ero s'orun lawa n'se"* (the title of a song he loved so much to sing). That is *we are pilgrims here on our way to heaven.* Thus he always had this urgent air about him, as if the Lord could break through the clouds any moment. Therefore Rev. Akindayomi was ever alert and brisk in his manners. He did everything as if there could be no time to do it tomorrow. If you were among Papa's workers, you must catch that urgency "bug" in him and work for the Lord with all sense of purpose. Workers were told that they must ever and always BE READY to get the heavenly call at ANY TIME. The workers heard it from him at every opportunity that they must be holy, prayerful and diligent in their walk with the Lord.

As a result of Papa's discipline his church workers consisted of only those who had made up their minds to serve his kind of God. They had so imbibed his spirit of punctuality that no one came late to church. As a matter of fact, the last persons to arrive workers' meeting could not talk for the first ten minutes of their arrival. Why? Their breath would still be short from running with all their strength! Many got in and quickly removed their shirts in order to squeeze out the sweat, because probably they had run all the way from the nearest bus stop (Oyingbo) until they entered the auditorium at Ebute-Metta. It was a race for life.

Papa's style of appointing workers and Pastors was quite unique. You never knew when the call would come. Papa personally observed people without their knowing - zeal, commitment, prayer fervency, etc. Oftentimes during general congregational prayers, Papa went round tapping certain individuals and telling them to come into the vestry for further prayers after the service. You arrived that inner sanctuary to discover that you had been elevated either unto a worker or a pastor. No one ever knew when it was coming. However once Papa has brought you in you are in, and you better sit up! For the old man applying the rod did not stop with his natural children. When it was necessary Papa caned his church members too, especially pastors and workers. The race of heaven was for the prepared.

The story was told of a certain brother who was a church worker. He was engaged to be married, but before the marriage could be solemnised, he had impregnated his fiancee. The matter came to Papa's notice. The first step was that Papa gave him some strong lashes of the cane. Secondly he was barred from being in the Workers' meeting nor doing any work in church. His punishment was for the next eight weeks. However he must report with the other workers at the normal time, but he was to sit outside the auditorium from that early morning till end of service. It wouldn't matter if it rained cats and dogs or the sun shone like a furnace. In Papa's lifetime this brother eventually became a pastor with the Redeemed Christian Church of God, and a committed one at that.

MODE OF WORSHIP
Interestingly, despite coming out of the Aladura church setting, noted for much music, clapping and dancing, Papa's new church was a radical departure from his white

garment background.

Here church life was much more solemn and regimented. The central theme was holiness and for Papa Akindayomi this translated into no clapping, dancing, (instruments of music nor accompaniments). Don't forget that he had had some interaction with the Apostolic Faith Church also, with their equally stern orientation. No doubt, their influence rubbed off on Papa to an extent. Although he was a deep worshipper and he taught his church to worship, but no form of dance suggestion was permitted as part of worship. The church choir was only exposed to violin training from the Apostolic Faith Church. Otherwise they did their ministrations without any other kind of musical instruments. Thus service was solemn, sober and somehow intimidating for some. The sombre nature of the church made it quite unattractive to a majority of people, who would only run in when they needed help.

STORM IN A TEACUP
& THE WAILING WAILERS

If you were in Papa's church and took his teachings to heart you could never be a wimpy Christian at all. Papa prayed and taught his people to pray. Not always keen on unserious members who only came around for miracles or to be prayed for, Papa rather demonstrated before his people how to cultivate the spirit of prayer. He made his church to realise that sin was an enemy of prayer.

Thus if you aspire to have prayer results you must hate

sin with a passion. Papa did not just teach this, he lived it before his people. His blazing eyes convicted you instantly when you had sinned.

Prayer in Papa's church was not a "refined" affair at all. Since you must use your own mouth to "pray through" for yourself, prayer time was thus very loud, noisy and quite emotional. To call the next prayer point, the conductor would have to use a hand bell. It was a common sight during prayer to see people weeping, crying and wailing loudly for sin or other matters as they called upon God. *"Praying through"* was the attitude of continuing in prayer after the day's sermon until you were certain that you had settled with God any area of your life touched by the message. As a result the after message prayers were never conclusive. Nobody prayed for anybody. Each person responded to God in personal prayer. Whenever anyone was satisfied that they had *"prayed through"* they left. This style of prayer still subsists with the Deeper Life Bible church.

Since praying through varied with individuals it was not a strange sight at church then, to see some people who started praying along with the others immediately after the morning service, still there on their faces when the church reconvened for the evening service at 6.00 p.m. That meant they had not *"prayed through."* Same for salvation prayer. When a sinner had repented of his sins, he was left at the altar to keep praying until he had prayed through unto the assurance of salvation. That aspect of sorrow for sin manifested in weeping and crying, earned Papa's church (and others like it), the appellation of 'The Wailing Church' (i.e. Ijo awon elekun). The general belief of the outsiders was that all these people ever went to church to do was just to go and weep all day.

But if you came to Papa's church and you wept your way unto his altar, the glory cloud rested upon your life and you never went back unto a life of sin. Your conversion was deep and thorough. Apart from the noise and the wailing, the congregation was taught also to pray with the knowledge of the Scriptures. This was to ensure that they not only prayed according to the will of God but also announce to the devil that they knew their rights as children of God. Papa abhorred ignorance of Scriptures. After all he knew what that had caused him early in life.

CHURCH LIFE: ORGANIC WHOLE
Like the first Apostolic Community of Acts, Church life in Rev. Akindayomi's church was very communal. Papa took his responsibility as a spiritual father very seriously. No one was left in doubt that there was a father in the house, who also cared about their natural lives too. Papa supervised every area of your life; and never apologised for it. His fathering had strength in it.

MARRIAGE
Papa's approach to marriage was not only spiritual but very practical too. For him spirituality was correctly positioned when practical realities on ground were also not taken for granted. When a young man had showed

interest in a young lady and the church authorities had been duly informed, then the long journey into the marriage act begins. No one was allowed to assume. An intending bridegroom's passbook or bank account was checked to know whether he had enough to prosecute the wedding ceremony and cater to immediate responsibilities afterwards. The bride's gown must have been submitted to the church authorities for inspection and approval before the wedding day. The gown must be so simple that the bride could wear it as a normal dress afterwards.

Papa or any other leader of the church must not hear it that a new bridegroom went a-borrowing after the marriage ceremony. Thus part of the laid down law before marriage approval was that there be no elaborate ceremonies necessitating needless spending. Each couple was only to do as they were able. No more, no less.

Papa wanted the Marriage Committee to find out if the intending bridegroom had a bed, some furnishing to start a home with, a stove and a few crockery. If his answer was positive then he was qualified to proceed into marriage. Papa used to disagree with those who would claim to want to do it "by faith," yet with nothing at all on ground. No matter how persuaded they claimed to be, Papa would refuse them. Members of the opposite sex (whether in courtship or not) were not permitted to visit each other clandestinely. Those whose courtship had been approved by the church, met and talked in the church or went to their leader's home. Papa believed that such close monitoring discouraged sin and the easy infiltration of Satan into the congregation.

An incident occurred once which convinced the people beyond a shadow of doubt that the old man meant everything and anything he ever told them: one of Papa's daughters somehow got impregnated by her husband-to-be while they were still courting. *Trouble!* When the story was told, Papa with very strong words promptly placed the errant daughter on suspension-she was to come to church but sit outside the auditorium for a certain number of months, and everyone was told what her offence was. As for the man responsible, Papa publicly called him up too in the congregation. With the finger of God, Papa pointed at him that day and said, *"you...!"* That was as far as he got-the fellow tumbled over violently under the power of God. Nobody touched him. There was palpable fear of the living God in the whole assembly that day. What next? Hope not another Ananias and Sapphira scene? The man laid on the floor for the next several hours, under terrible conviction and dealing from the Lord. Afterwards he also received his own suspension term.

Interestingly, after each service, Papa found time to identify with the fellow, opening the Word of God with him, talking to him, and encouraging him to co-operate with God by serving out his punishment faithfully and without grumbling because that was the path of eternal life.

The stories have it that it took personal forgiveness and prayers of intercession by Papa for his daughter to deliver her baby safely eventually-the pregnancy went beyond nine months! Papa had been most unhappy with his beloved daughter for her untoward behaviour. Now when a man would deal with his own household like that, with what manner of hand suppose ye that he would handle God's heritage under his care? He was by all means their Papa. Everyone of them knew that, but his charity began from right under his own roof.

A WEDDING CEREMONY

At this early time also another story was told of when one of Papa's own daughters got married at the church. The church auditorium was under construction then and the work was being done by communal effort. Already the people were aware that wedding reception was never elaborate in their church. So they knew what to expect. What they never planned for however was Papa not sparing even his visiting in-laws and their guests.

Immediately after the marriage ceremony, the reception was made very brief. Papa sent the new couple home and ordered everybody else back to work on site! To prove that he meant business he had the church gates locked. Papa's in-laws hardly believed their eyes. The bride's mother-in-law was so devastated that she wept cats and dogs that day. But Papa seemed not to notice. He personally supervised the work on site and made sure everyone worked.

SPECIAL DEDICATIONS

Whether baby dedication, naming, house dedication and the like, Papa discouraged elaborate ceremonies. Thus child naming was done very early in the morning with the new parents bringing their baby and a few packets of biscuits for sharing afterwards. From there those going to work left directly to their places of work. During the dedication, Papa would admonish the parents that monies given them was for the baby and not for the adults' personal enjoyment and indulgence.

It was the church practice after a woman's delivery to send women in groups of two's or more to take care of the new mother and baby. The women helped in going to market, cooking, and housekeeping until the new mother was strong enough to resume work and church attendance.

SECRET POLICE

Papa's close nephew, Ebenezer Olufemi Ademulegun (*presently a pastor with the RCCG*) , then a young man, had a dose of his uncle's close monitoring one day. His wife had given birth and it was the day of the baby's naming. Very early in the morning before anyone arrived, Papa showed up in Ebenezer's house. Everyone was shocked at Papa's sudden appearance at such "*unholy*" hour and without any prior notice. Papa's reply was that he was "*just passing by*" and thought to say "hello."

But Ebenezer got to know better when Papa headed

straight for his refrigerator as if he needed a drink of water. The old man was peering. Then it dawned on him: Papa had actually come to do a gum-shoe's work. He wanted to catch his nephew red-handed if he had loaded the fridge with alcoholic beverage to celebrate his baby's naming! If he had mentioned his coming the young man may have adjusted his acts. Therefore Papa's unannounced visit was his way of telling you he could never be deceived by any of his children-natural or spiritual. They all knew that with Papa, anything was possible. So the name of the game was-be ready!

FUNERALS

Church members were discouraged from doing elaborate funeral ceremonies, as is wont to be if one's dead parents were old. In the Western part of Nigeria here the culture is to spend big and cook plenty and make a lot of noise in order to show that you were happy to survive your parents. But inasmuch as Papa encouraged children to have befitting burials for their late parents they were not to engage in needless spending sprees. The popular Lagos style of *"turning the other side"* of a dead loved one was certainly frowned at. This involves buying of expensive fabrics, elaborate fanfare and sometimes excessive eating, drinking and revelling in an unmistakable party spirit. Papa's opinion was that true heavenly minded Christians ought to do things in moderation, because carousing is sin.

HOUSE WARMING/DEDICATION

When a member had built a house (personal,

commercial, etc) and informed the church it was never a noisy affair. A few men among the elders were delegated to go and pray on the house, dedicating it unto the Lord. There was no party or any other ceremony afterwards.

FAMILY LIFE

Papa was not so spiritual as to neglect the life of the natural body. After all the Word of God says, **"Howbeit that was not first which is spiritual, but that which is natural, and afterward that which is spiritual"** (1 Corinthians 15: 46).

Papa Akindayomi believed that if the physical body was healthy and well taken care of, it would be primed for utmost spiritual productivity as well. Thus as he teaches his congregation to pray, to fast, to serve God, he also taught them about family life. Papa would tell his people that the best form of family planning for couples was abstinence. When you are not ready for another baby there is no need to indulge yourselves in too much sex. You could channel your physical energies in other more productive and creative ways. And for Papa, a wise woman was not ready to nurse another baby until the last one was nearing two years of age.

A HOME - PAGE

One of Papa's natural daughters once had the tongue lashing of her life along with the husband right from Papa's pulpit one day. What happened? The young woman's last baby was less than a year old, and to Papa's shock she was pregnant again.

Papa did not rebuke her quietly under the roof. He made her a public example by mentioning her and the husband as part of his sermon on a particular Sunday. Quite unfortunately the child eventually died before the new one was born. Papa denounced his daughter and son-in-law publicly again from the pulpit saying that this couple *killed* their own baby; by not allowing it to be properly nurtured and weaned before making another one. They felt bad and were both ashamed.

OFFERING/GIVING
The early life of The Redeemed Christian Church of God was not a prosperous one by any means. The little flock believed in and practised much sacrificial living and giving. Whatever was to be done in the church had to be done sacrificially. The people would give up whatever they had to meet urgent needs-money, property, personal possessions, time, etc. It was quite easy for instance for those who had T. V. sets to sell them because the church doctrine at this period was opposed to television. It was thought to be *"the devil's box."* People sold bicycles, cars, anything and brought the money into the Lord's house. It was on record that at this critical time Pastor E. A. Adeboye, *(present General Overseer of the RCCG)* , also sold his own car at a point and submitted the proceeds to the church.

At another time, not knowing that it was part of the tests the Lord had set to further confirm the next leader of the church; Pastor E. A. Adeboye responded to Papa's directive that every one of the leaders should close their bank accounts and bring the money, because the church had an urgent need. To all intents and purposes everyone concerned did; but on investigation even Adeboye himself was shocked to discover that he alone had complied completely with that call. The others hid some and brought some. As a rule Papa was known to be less keen on being spoilt with gifts from people. He always wanted his church to be blessed materially but you could not do it clandestinely either. For example when people brought large gifts they were quizzed about the state of their soul, what they did for a living, etc.

The quality of a giver's life and testimony was of big interest. If Papa was not sure of the fruit of righteousness in someone's life he discouraged their giving to the work. New comers were particularly barred whenever special needs arose in the church. Papa wanted to know the standing of such new people first before joining their hands to the plough. He had the same attitude to the collection of tithes and special offerings. During this early period when the congregation had become large enough to need public address gadgets, Papa made the needs known to the church and left it at that.

On one glorious Sunday like that the people arrived church to see a set of beautiful brand new amplifier and one or two other items donning a corner of the altar. *Great!* Unknown to them Papa had earlier been intimated with the generous donation, and he had wanted to know the giver. He was told. The snag in the whole matter however was that the gentleman who presented these things to the church, even though quite well-to-do, was yet neither here nor there in the profession of his faith-Jesus was not yet completely Lord over his life-he still lived with two wives. On that note Papa would not permit his gift to be used upon the Lord's altar. Therefore during service that day Papa talked directly to his faithful church member- *"man, this is not what the Lord requires at your hands, but your total repentance for the salvation of your soul."* [1]

The message that day was that the Lord could not truly bless partial obedience. What! The man broke down under terrible conviction, and ended up repenting totally and making Jesus Lord over his entire affairs. He wept his way into the Kingdom. More was to come: as they arrived home after service, his second wife quietly without prodding from anyone went about packing all her things, and afterwards came and told her husband, *"I've discovered my true position and realised my state now, I'm not supposed to be in your house. I'll be on my way."* [2] And the woman left.

Not a few felt that Rev. Akindayomi was carrying things to the extreme, and many even called him a fool. But his ever ready answer always was that the way of the cross was foolishness, especially to the perishing! The man of God never relented from the straight and narrow path concerning even this sensitive issue because for him, the way of the cross was the believer's sure path to glory.

A recurring character trait many close associates

repeatedly pointed out about Papa Akindayomi was that the man was completely uninterested in material things. They held no attractions for him whatsoever. If God did not say yes he would not take a gift, no matter what it was. Some he would tell to take their gifts or offerings to the church. He was extremely selective about personal gifts, and most of what he received was converted to church use, including lands.

A TYPICAL SUNDAY

Having attained some level of stability, church life became quite organised and certain things automatically fell into place with time. Church workers and pastors ended their own prayers and flowed into the normal congregational prayer which began around 7:00 am. Prayer was a do-it-yourself affair and people prayed fervently with all their heart. The sermon was long or short depending upon the move of the Spirit and prayers could be interspersed in-between. Morning service closed around 2:00 p.m., but people did not go home. There was evangelism coupled with follow-up of new converts and new comers. Every one took it as if it was their personal business.

Papa's usual admonition to the people was that any opportunity they had to serve the Lord was a time of grace. It might not be there tomorrow because the Lord could show up before the morrow. That was his mind set. Thus he kept his people permanently on their toes serving the Lord. He had the same opinion about praying, especially for sinners. To neglect to pray for a sinner daily was to lose an opportunity to serve the Lord.

Those who had issues accruing from the morning sermon to settle with the Lord, remained behind praying through while the others trooped out for various assignments for God. They returned for the evening service which could last till well after 7:00 p.m. On a typical Sunday, a faithful Redeemed Church member hardly got home before 8:00 or 9:00 p.m. But everyone served with joy and gladness.

SALVOS FROM HELL

While Rev. Akindayomi prayed for people left, right and centre and it was miracles galore, the man faced personal challenges and serious trials of his faith at the home front; but which were not permitted to derail him, distract him nor slow him down in any way. He had embraced the call and surely there was a price to pay for such a high calling in God. The enemy kept firing fiery arrows from different directions but with grim determination and his face set like flint the man of God progressed on the journey.

TRAGEDY AT HOME

Not too long after leaving the C&S and starting the "Ogo Oluwa" Fellowship, Papa had his first taste of pain. Tragedy struck at home. His first son, Joshua (second child of the house) suffered a sudden attack while Mama was feeding him. The illness which started as convulsion resulted in permanent brain damage to the child. Joshua was always an invalid and was bedfast for most of his life on earth before finally passing away years later. While alive prayer warriors were stationed with him round the clock, either at home or in the church. On his "attack" days Joshua would urinate or defecate at the same spot on his bed. Thus his room, bedding and clothes constantly needed to be scrubbed and washed with very strong antiseptic. Some days he would just "go off" as if in an epileptic seizure. And after a while the fit would lift and he would be normal again. On his "normal" days he would play football with his friends and generally be happy. But it never lasted. Soon the attacks were back again. This became a "normal" part of Papa's family's life from 1945 until Joshua finally died in 1969, aged 25.

Now on the day that Joshua would die Papa was billed to travel to Ibadan. He was involved in a lot of travelling at this period because his young church was just beginning to establish out of town parishes, and so Papa went on evangelistic campaigns often.

Before stepping out that day Papa checked on Joshua as usual, but coming out of Joshua's room he called his household and informed them that God just told him Joshua would die before he returns. Nobody in the house must raise alarm or cry to attract any undue attention. Papa particularly warned Mama Egbedire (*the child's mother*) strictly. Afterwards Papa sent for the church's physician, Dr Alakija, and said to him: *"I see that Joshua would be dead before I come back and as the church doctor I know it will be your duty to check him and write the death certificate. Now I charge you to record exactly whatever be* the cause of his death. Don't try to hide anything." [3] The doctor was aghast! Why should Papa be so sure that somebody would die just like that? His own child? And he was so matter-of-factly about it? Dr. Alakija impressed it on Papa that even he as a trained doctor couldn't give such a final word. After all Papa is not a doctor. Papa said, *"Don't worry, this one will die, but because he will be buried in my absence that's why I'm giving everyone their own instructions before I leave. Write the death certificate accordingly. Let it be known what killed him."* [4] With final instructions to church elders for Joshua's burial Papa picked up his evangelist's bag and hat and left on his missionary journey. Everything happened as he had told his people. He had ordered that all of Joshua's personal effects be buried with him, while the bedding and other stuff in his room were to be burnt. The instructions were carried out accordingly.

On the minute that Joshua stopped breathing in Lagos, Papa told the people with him in Ibadan: *"My son Joshua just passed away at home,"* then he continued what he was saying to them.

Interestingly, before Joshua, Papa's first child ever, a baby boy also, born after four years of Esther Egbedire's waiting for the fruit of the womb, lived only thirty days (one month) after birth and then died. Joshua was his second child. But despite this serious trial of his faith, Papa went on fervently serving the Lord. He never despaired. It never crossed Papa's mind to query God why his own lot should be like that despite being a "miracle man"to so many distressed people, especially in the area of conception and miraculous deliveries. And unquestionably he's a prophet of God. As a matter of fact Papa himself in reminiscence of those trying times had this to say: "...it is not possible to suppose that simply because we have accepted Christ there should be no trials. Whosoever the Lord has called should just make up their mind that whatever may come they would not deny Jesus." [5]

Papa believed in faith healing, even back at the C&S. Thus he never used drugs nor permitted them into his home. As a result, all through his sickness Joshua was never taken to hospital. At a point when Papa's family intervened, and threatened him with legal action should the boy die, Papa did not relent. His people felt he was carrying the "religion thing" too far, but Papa made it known to them that the child was his; dead or alive. If the Lord healed him and he lived, great. But if the Lord did not heal him, and he died, that was fine by him also. Papa told his people that whether he took his son to hospital or not would not avail if it was God's will for him to die and not live.

When Papa's extended family visited after Joshua's passing away, Papa told them point blank that God gave and He had taken away. He knew best. It was not possible for a Christian to only expect good things on earth and never experience bad things. We are on earth as spiritual pilgrims and certain things happen to try our faith. He made his family realise also that his son was not lost, but had merely gone ahead of him to heaven. They would surely meet again. After this confrontation no family people troubled him again.

As for his household, Papa's strength transfused into everyone and thus they remained strong. For Papa however, that was just a chapter of his life closed. He was already into the very next one.

DEATH OF THE TWO DEJIS

Papa buried another son sometime after Joshua. This second son, *(fourth in the family)* Deji, died quite young. Deji, aged five, died on Wednesday, a fellowship day. As a matter of fact Papa had seen signs somehow that the boy would die. But nothing could happen to make him not go to church on a fellowship day. So he called Mama and told her that the signs he was seeing showed that Deji would not last that night. As soon as he passes away Mama Egbedire was to dress him, cover the corpse and go to her sister's place until Papa would come back at night. As usual, he told her, *"no noise!"* Everything happened as Papa had said and Mama did as she was told, doing her best to comfort Deji's siblings in the house.

When the entire household was back together that night, Papa went in to check on the dead child but his face betrayed nothing when he came out. Afterwards Papa personally made the eba (cassava meal) for that evening and served everyone, commanding them to eat. It was while at table that a concerned neighbour, an elderly woman came in to mourn with the family, but she met the entire household eating. Incredible!

The dead child was just in the next room across. The confused woman was at a loss for what to say, therefore she left in quiet wonder. Thus Papa trudged on and never for once permitted the fiery darts of the enemy to pierce his shield of faith.

After this episode, another son was born and named Deji because he looked so much like the former one. This Deji who died in 1978, just two years before Papa's passing away was aged 21. He was already working with Leventis Motors at this time. Recalling that particular incident, Papa's last son, Pastor Ifeoluwa Akindayomi said: *"Brother Deji and Papa were very close because he was a very kind and dutiful son. I remember he bought our first fridge in the house then. I think his own death particularly affected Papa rather badly because it was after it that he started getting tired in his body."* [6]

In his lifetime Rev Akindayomi buried a total number of six children; the very last one, some seven months before his own final home call.

One thing that every one who ever lived with Rev. Akindayomi under the same roof, or interacted with him at close quarters embraced unconsciously was that bull-dog determination to keep faith with God, no matter what. The man's philosophy was that whatever happens you must resolutely follow the Lord. Heaven will compensate for the present tears because the Lord is faithful. According to Papa's children, this attitude to life affected Mama Akindayomi in such a manner that she supervised the children to always carefully observe Papa's likes and dislikes and follow his ways.

Her submission to Papa was total.

NOTES

1) Interview with Pastor Ebenezer Ademulegun
2) Ibid.,
3) Interview with Pastor (Mrs.) Olukowajo
4) Ibid.,
5) From Rev. J. O. Akindayomi's memoirs
6) Interview with Pastor Ifeoluwa Akindayomi

CHAPTER FOUR

THE MAN

JOSIAH OLUFEMI AKINDAYOMI

REV. JOSIAH OLUFEMI AKINDAYOMI from what we have seen so far was definitely a consummate human being. You never met him once and ever forgot the experience. He was the kind of character people call memorable. When he meets you he leaves you with a certain impression: you either love him or you hate him. This was a man who did nothing by half nor got involved in anything half heartedly. If he was in he was in and if he was out you were not left in doubt where he stood.

In this chapter we would be exploring some of the dynamics that constituted the make-up of the man Josiah Olufemi Akindayomi. What made him tick? What were his personality traits? How did people who interacted with him see him? Let's continue this journey of discovery.

THIRST FOR KNOWLEDGE

You may like to ask, if it had never crossed your mind before, how did a man like Abram hear God? What language did God speak? Did Abram hear with his ears or his heart? What's the difference? What did the voice of God sound like? These questions become interesting and relevant in the light of the fact that there seems to be such similarity between the call of father Abraham and that of Rev. J. O. Akindayomi; which makes a comparison of their two lives worth examining critically.

They both were born, bred and raised in complete idolatry. They had no heritage of godliness in their immediate family, yet God found in them the kind of heart that He could use. Therefore He called them right out of unapologetic idolatry and their world benefitted by their unflinching obedience.

For a man like Rev. Akindayomi what had been the interesting poser is the fact that he definitely was not and could not have been the only "convert" at the time of his first contact with Christianity, so how come he shone so distinctly? If you have noticed the style of conversion at this point in the history of British West Africa, it was not always a total affair. Often a Sangodeyi or Ifamuyiwa liked the (gospel)stories of the white missionaries, and out of curiosity agreed to follow them.

His zeal and interest were unmistakable but "church" was for Sundays. The other days of the week were for the "normal" things of old like it had been even before the supposed conversion. Thus in order to establish their belief that Christianity was a "different affair" from their traditional ways, our grandfathers had songs like:

Awa o s'oro ile wa o/2x
Igbagbo o pe,
O yee
Igbagbo o pe k'awa ma s'oro
Awa o s'oro ile wa o.

That is, *"Christianity is no reason for us to abandon our fathers' traditional ways, surely we must celebrate our traditional heritage."* Under this 'anointing' you subsequently saw a John Egundeyi donning his father's *egungun* (masquerade) gear and chanting the invocation of the spirits on a festival day.

That's for the gods of the fathers. On Sunday the same fellow will wear his Sunday best and head for church! He may even be a chorister or an usher. It wasn't supposed to make any difference. Conversions were not radical to the point of leaving all and coming completely clean. It's a fact of our contemporary history that our early African orthodox clergy, (using Ezekiel 20:20 as cover); introduced Ogboni Fraternity, and the different Lodges into the church; personally recruiting prominent individuals in their congregations as members.

However, one observes, as was with father Abraham also that Rev. J. O. Akindayomi personally heard the voice of the almighty God distinctly in the midst of such thick darkness and recognised it apart! That sounds dramatic, and quite incredible. This was a man so entrenched in darkness that at a time he was even a consulting native doctor.

No man could speak to Saul of Tarsus concerning Christ. He was too strong in his spirit. His involvement and commitment in the Jewish religion made him a dangerous antagonist of the early Christians. The Jewish Christians would rather avoid him than have anything to do with Saul. Yet that was a mighty vessel for the Kingdom's cause. God left Saul to zealously continue in his wrong ways until He was ready for him. From the point of his dramatic conversion all through his life as a servant of God Paul always heard the voice of his God.

Men hardly featured in the life of Paul as [his] instructors or teachers. And this we have discovered from Scriptures and Church history to be the stamp of authentic apostolic ministry. God directly instructing an individual and giving them a specific assignment to do for Him. This trait is so clear in the call and ministry of Rev. J.O Akindayomi. Having no man to copy or follow, his sensitivity to God's voice was razor sharp .

Abraham would move from this point to that one and build an altar. In a short while he had moved again. The man kept moving as his God kept directing him. When Hagar and Ishmael would go; when he would receive the instruction for circumcision; when his name would be changed from Abram to Abraham; no man told

Abraham what to do, neither did he have anyone to copy or learn from. Men like that hardly are men followers. They are individuals with a questing heart, even in the midst of their dark surroundings. On the day that a different *Being* showed up on his own dial also, Akindayomi recognised that this was the God he had been serving in ignorance! And he jumped at the offer of a walk with the true God.

One of the expected characteristics of an uneducated person should be timidity or some level of timorousness. But not for Akindayomi at all. The moment the light of the Gospel had shined into his heart, albeit imperfectly he instantly began to run with it in search of a better understanding. This kind of pilgrimage, questing heart became the bedrock of all that we saw the man eventually becoming in the hand of the Almighty God.

In His earthly days, our Lord Jesus Christ castigating the Jews for their lukewarmness and hardness of heart once said unto them, **"Woe unto thee, Chorazin! Woe unto thee, Bethsaida! For if the mighty works, which were done in you, had been done in Tyre and Sidon, they would have repented long ago in sackcloth and ashes"** (Matthew 11: 21). Akindayomi not only repented in *"dust and ashes,"* but he ran in the direction of the little glimpse of light showed to him. As a result of his diligent and determined pursuit the scope began to widen and expand, until the Sun of righteousness had captured his whole heart.

Before the outbreak of the "S. U" revival of the early 70's in Nigeria, the C&S Church Movement of Orimolade had been around for ages. Orimolade had been involved in evangelistic campaigns since 1918 with phenomenal signs and wonders following his ministry. Thus the C&S influence and practice was already quite strong and popular before other Gospel churches came along. The C&S believed in and practiced faith healing, visions, dreams, prophecies, exorcism, etc. Many of our grandmothers and grandfathers were quite familiar with the *"Aladura Church"* phenomenon in their time. Aladura became so popular, Nobel Laureate Wole Soyinka wrote about it in his *Jero Plays*. The Orimolade Movement drew massive crowds back then, and everyone seemed to know *Olorun Orimolade* (i.e. the God of Orimolade).

Having left the orthodox side to join the Charismatic Movement, Papa Akindayomi was never one to sit on the sidelines and watch others take all the action. He was ever a pro-active man. God kept adding to his knowledge, wisdom and maturity over the years, while He kept telling him, *"I have an assignment for you, but not in this place,"* and he kept following one step at a time, patiently moving with the Lord.

Having spoken to a number of Rev. Akindayomi's family and close relations, many have lamented nostalgically that they wished the man had been educated. But you know what? It was not impossible or difficult for the Almighty God to have sovereignly arranged his formal education if He had so wanted it. After all God sovereignly "arranged" for the erudite Saul of Tarsus to study under the very best of the Law teachers of his time (see Acts 5:34;22:3). Saul would never have known as an unbeliever why he had to study under such a fine teacher as Gamaliel, but God knew! Therefore to my mind, and in the light of the foregoing, Rev. Akindayomi was the best he could have been for God despite his perceived limitations. His lack of Western education did not in any way reduce or take away from God's anointing that rested upon him. He paid the price and God connected him to power. American apostle and evangelist, Dr. John G. Lake (1870-1935), mentioned in a sermon titled 'The Power of God,' that *"Man's intellectuality is not an assistance to knowing God."* [1] And how true! Rev. J. O. Akindayomi is an incontrovertible proof of that fact. By the way how learned were most of the Apostles of the Lamb? Check Acts 4:13.

That which God wanted Akindayomi to do he did excellently well and without fail. And I hope you and I are aware that true Apostolic ministry is all about accuracy, not necessarily about works. When he would die apostle Paul said, **"I have finished my course,"** and beloved, it was a cry of triumph. When the Lord Jesus was now stretched thin on the cross and His enemies were busy mocking, the Son of God cried out to heaven and said, **"it is finished!"**

Instantly heaven began to rejoice, for that was a signal of

total victory. Until Jesus uttered that cry His spirit could not depart His body despite all the agony and trauma of crucifixion. It is written that God is no respecter of persons. When Rev. Akindayomi would depart, he told his people, "by this time tomorrow, everywhere there's a Redeemed parish you will all be rejoicing and giving glory to God." Why? His job was done here and heaven had confirmed that fact to him. There is so much that our own highly educated, highly strung-up, pressure cooker, micro-wave, generation can learn as lessons in diligence, patience and faithfulness from this uneducated apostle of God. For it is written, **"for he that cometh to God must believe that he is, and that He is a rewarder of them that diligently seek Him"** (Hebrews 11:6b). The key-word here is diligence. Diligence is something which not only takes time but necessarily demands that you pay strict attention to details, no matter how little.

Papa Akindayomi sought God with a very high sense of diligence and we all are witnesses today and beneficiaries of his reward. He truly painstakingly sought after God.

In the Bible we have seen the pattern of the Apostolic as portrayed in the ministries of Noah the Ark builder (Gen. 6: 13-16); Moses the Tabernacle builder (Ex. 25:9, 26:30); David who instructed Solomon concerning the building of the Temple (I Chr. 28: 9-13). In all these cases you will discover the Spirit of God giving detailed and specific instructions about materials, measurements, and even the kind of men to do the assigned work. This is God's eternal pattern which no man can change or alter.

STRONG SPIRITUAL LEADER

"He was a man of prayer. He was a strong spiritual leader." Those were the opening words of Pastor J. A. O Akindele, a son-in-law to Papa Akindayomi and a foundation member of the RCCG, about the man Akindayomi.

The strength of a true spiritual leader rests in their ability to separate emotions from spiritual reality. Papa Akindayomi was much a man of God's presence, which translates to a heavy abiding of God's Spirit with him all the time. The man was a moving house of prayer.

Much beloved by all and sundry for his loving and fatherly attributes, but then everyone knows that Papa was not someone you trifled with when it comes to spiritual things. According to Pastor (Mrs.) O. O. Akindele *(Papa's second daughter) "Papa had a kind of awe about him which made people to fear him, even his own children." "We were never frivolous around him at all." "When you were around Papa you became more conscious of heaven than of anything else." "The fervency of his spirit after the Lord affected anyone who came close to him."*

Probably from his early days of poverty and lack, or as a result of deliberate spiritual discipline, but after starting his own church, Papa lived a fasted life. To take off initially he went on a six-month fast. Afterwards his normal style was to eat one major meal a day and that was in the evening. He loved pounded yam and bush meat. He also had a tradition of a yearly 40-day fast at a go during which he ate no food at all but drank only water, yet he went about his normal duties and appointments. He showed no signs of strain or fatigue. Apart from this long fast, Papa also went on different kinds of fasting as God's Spirit would lead him. Sometimes it was three (3) or seven (7) or fourteen (14) or twenty-one (21) days. While still with the C&S he often had personal prayer retreats at the beach during which time he saw nobody; but spent the whole time alone with God.

Being a much meditative person who spent long periods in God's presence, Papa was a man of quite few words. In the words of Papa's first daughter, Pastor (Mrs.) Olukowajo: *"Papa's prayer for people was often short, because he spends such long hours in God's presence. His pronouncements were more of commands. And they happened accordingly."*

According to reports, his moods depended on the Holy Spirit's dealing with him. On *"happy"* days, Papa arrived the church and noticed virtually everyone around, greeted them and exchanged pleasantries, even with people outside his church gates. But on *"red rag"* days he came out of the house moody, uncommunicative and not too friendly even with his driver in the car. On such days Papa walked briskly past anyone on his path greeting nobody and headed straight for his office. If you are wise, that's a day to steer totally clear of the man.

The very look on his face was dreadful! Close associates say on such days, God was probably saying something very serious to His servant and you dare not divert his attention. He was totally concentrated on the Spirit.

When Papa was still growing his church, the laws and doctrines were strong and strict. All kinds of people came to church. And some used to complain that their services were like a funeral: dancing, clapping, drums, and instruments of music were not allowed. Rather than bend to the "popular" temper, Papa responded by making church membership or attendance not compulsory. He said those who did not like his style were free to go, but those who were interested in going to heaven should stay and follow God with him. The leader's fear of people leaving him was never a part of his thought pattern.

He was also known to be extremely intolerant of sin or any form of slackness. Therefore it mattered less to him who was caught in any misdemeanour, and punishment was public. Thus discipline reigned supreme in his church members. Many for the fear of public rebuke and discipline chose to stay away from sin!

On some Sundays, Papa would run his hand through his snow white hair as the service was progressing, and he would not smile at all. Any day his people saw that, the congregation was extra nice in their behaviour. That was not a day to relax at any point! Just be on your toes. Don't dose. Don't mistakenly whisper to your friend next to you. Do not by any means have a reason to stand up to go to the toilet at the wrong time, nor scratch your shoes noisily on the floor. There could be an explosion! Papa's people knew his signs and interpreted them accurately. If he had things on his mind that God was telling him for his people, he hated any form of distraction.

One of Papa's very close aides, a foundation member, an elder and actually one of the comfortable ones among his people; had a taste of Papa's sore nerves one day. Papa had called for an emergency worker's meeting and told them to be there at 2.00 p.m. It was a Sunday. This elderly man and his wife came in when it was long past two o'clock. When they arrived Papa ordered the doors to be locked against them, and exclaimed: *"the outside is for dogs,..."* On that note he continued with the workers' meeting, and informed the ones sitting before him that blessing a servant of God with a car or a house or whatsoever else had nothing to do with pleasing God and making heaven. Obviously this man was in good financial standing with the church, but Papa said to get to heaven you had to abide by God's principles regardless of what you gave to God's work. He had no apology for the defaulting elder.

At this early period, Papa was also personally in charge of water baptism. He it was that conducted the rites for those to be baptised. On baptism day, a prospective Baptismal candidate was required to pray for two straight hours while standing. You were not to lean against the wall. While the prayer was going on, Papa was walking around supervising the proceedings. At the end of two full hours, those who had passed the test would be separated from those who showed signs of weakness and tiredness during the exercise. If you had leaned against the wall or stopped your prayer before official stop you were out. Water baptism used to be once a year then. That meant if you failed Papa's endurance test you had to wait again till next year. His people knew him to be eagle-eyed, meticulous and very alert. Thus if you were a slack character you either ran away from him or amended your ways. If you changed and imbibed Papa's spirit however you would excel in all other areas of your life.

Papa faced challenges to his leadership from certain quarters but God personally vindicated him.

MUTINY ATTEMPTS
The church had begun to expand and within a few years there were RCCG branches at Somolu (Lagos), Ondo (Papa's home town), Ibadan, (Oyo State), Ilorin (Kwara State) and Osogbo in Osun State. New people had started to stream in, and Papa's sphere of influence as a spiritual leader began to widen. He was no more the pastor of a little flock at the corner shop. The church had also begun to hold its own National Conventions now. Delegates would come to Lagos from the different States of the Federation.

Prior to that year's National Convention a curious

misunderstanding suddenly erupted between Papa and the Circuit Superintendent of the church. The two old men were quite close therefore the open rift was most surprising. Against all entreaties the Circuit Superintendent insisted on leaving the Ministers' conference and going back to his station. In a huff he beckoned to his (official) driver. The young man promptly jumped in the car ready to zoom off. But wait! Kick, pump, boot, shove, the car would not start. Master and driver got down and pushed the car along a considerable distance; still no dice. Now what to do? They subsequently abandoned the vehicle and took public transport back to their station. On arrival the angry leader called an urgent meeting of his assistants. At the end of their own consultations they called the available church members together and informed them that the Mother Church back at Lagos had excised them from the fold, and as a matter of fact did not even invite them to the National Convention going on right now in Lagos. As a result that same night they were going to start their own crusade campaign. The year was 1974.

Unknown to these people, Papa had dispatched a 4-man delegation to Ibadan the moment the Circuit Superintendent had left in the manner he did. Papa's delegation arrived to meet the church in the midst of its own deliberations. The congregation had no idea what was going on, only the leaders. The two sides of leadership sat together on the altar. The Lagos delegation wanted to know from the congregation why they were absent at the National Convention going on in Lagos. The people replied that their leaders had told them they were no more a part of the Mother Church. Lagos did not want them. Some others said they were told that Lagos had backslided so much and was now only operating in the flesh. It was almost becoming like another Babel. Everybody spoke different things, without anyone understanding anybody.

While the consultations were still going on, the leader of the revolt grabbed his Bible, stormed out of the church and never came back. Ministers and members loyal to him followed the man out. Subsequently the Lagos delegation assured the remaining people that Lagos had never at any time in the past or intending in the future to excise them from the Mother Church. However since there was freedom of choice and association, they were very free to choose whom they would follow. Their former pastor or Rev. J. O. Akindayomi, RCCG leader.

Thereafter the atmosphere in the congregation relaxed and the people quieted down. The Lagos delegation prayed for them and left. This problem greatly affected this first Ibadan parish of RCCG, and it took awhile for the membership to pick up again. Reports got to the remnant congregation the following day that their former leader had secured a church facility for himself close by and had started his proposed crusade. Papa never talked about this matter publicly beyond that point. Only the leaders involved knew about it.

With experiences such as this one Papa made sure

shortly before his home-going that he left nothing to chance. Thus before he would die, apart from having intimated the eldership of the RCCG with God's choice of Pastor E. A. Adeboye as the next leader and having personally transferred his mantle through that unforgettable prayer in America, Rev. Akindayomi still recorded his last words on that matter in an audio tape. The tape was personally handed over to a much trusted person in Mama Egbedire's presence with clear instructions *(on pain of dire consequences if any one tried to alter what was there)*, to see to it that it was faithfully handed over and played to the hearing of all concerned. The man faithfully did as Papa commanded him.

GOD'S SERVANT

"And Miriam and Aaron spake against Moses because of the Ethiopian woman whom he had married: for he had married an Ethiopian woman. And the anger of the LORD was kindled against them;...." (Numbers 12: 1, 9).

A report of a mutiny once came to Lagos from the Oshogbo parish of the church. Some fellows had banded together against the Parish Pastor. When Papa got the report he decided to show up personally to settle the problem. On his arrival at the church the leader of the rebellion had the church entrance barred against Papa. He insisted that the old man would not enter into the church. Papa refused to be angry. He tried all he could to reason with the errant church man but the man was adamant. When he would not relent Papa replied, *"well if truly I am the one called by the almighty God as the founder of this church, then I leave you to God. I will turn back here now and head for Lagos."* With that Papa made a U-turn and was soon on his way back home. However, before Papa would arrive Lagos, the mutiny leader had become leprous! He was covered with the affliction from head to toe. Nobody believed it. Papa had no idea what had happened.

The following day emissaries arrived from Oshogbo to see Papa on account of the afflicted man and plead for forgiveness. But Papa made them to understand that he had nothing to do with it as he neither cursed the man nor prayed against him. He told the emissaries that the One who afflicted the man was the God who owned the Church. Nothing availed for the man and he remained leprous until the day of his death.

THIS IS MY PARKING SPACE!
Even though he hardly got angry or uttered angry words, people feared to offend Papa. Even if he said nothing when you have made him unhappy, you still had to pray for God's mercy. An incident occurred one day close to Papa's church which frightened onlookers and further confirmed to the people that Papa was truly an unusual servant of God.

Papa had his usual parking space at the lot in front of his church. However most often before he arrived others had parked their cars on the street all the way from one end to the other, right up to the church walls, taking over his own parking space as well. The church workers often would warn the people and appeal to them to please spare Papa's own parking space at least. But all appeals seemed to fall on deaf ears. On this particular day, the scene was not different. When Papa arrived church his parking space had been taken up. He said nothing, but only made his driver slow down so he could get out of the car. Very carefully as if counting, Papa surveyed the array of cars parked from the very beginning to the end of the street, until his eyes rested on the very car usurping his parking space. On that day Leventis Motors was the culprit. The parked cars were all new Renault cars, probably meant for delivery somewhere. The pain of being denied his parking space was obvious on Papa's face but he made no comment. Calmly he walked away from the scene and straight into his office. His driver was at a loss where to get the car parked.

Papa's neighbours in the area who knew him went in search of the driver of the particular offending car. Having intimated the man with what kind of a person Papa was, the driver raced to the spot with intention to remove his vehicle. Alas! As soon as the man got in the car and started the engine his vehicle caught a strange fire and went up in flames. Since then no one in that vicinity would dare trespass into Papa's parking space. They would park everywhere else but at that particular spot.

IGUNNU MISS ROAD!

It was very early in the morning around 7.00 a.m. The *Igunnu* (a kind of masquerade) party emerged from the opposite end of Papa's street. People were in different stages of early morning rituals in front of their houses. Some tying their loincloth and washing their cars, others perusing the morning papers, some others brushing their teeth, especially in the local style with chewing stick. The Igunnu company got closer to Papa's house. Papa was lounging on his verandah upstairs; not seeming to show interest in the different scenes around him. As the Igunnu company moved along the street, people ran in for fear while the bold ones quickly paid obeisance and continued staying outside to watch the masquerade. When Igunnu is passing in front of your house that early in the morning you were to remove your shoes, if you had a chewing stick in your mouth, you threw it away and were in an attitude of reverence and respect for the cult of the Igunnu.

Papa's driver happened to be in front of the house downstairs that day preparing to clean the car. He tied a loincloth and was vigorously cleaning his teeth with his big chewing stick. Incidentally he had on his bathroom slippers as well. The young man was quite oblivious of the Igunnu taboos, and clearly he had contravened all. The company got closer and he made no move to comply with their rule. Some of the Igunnu outriders ran towards him, and in their impressive guttural voices ordered him to respect the Igunnu. How? The young man did not know. They made signs to him what they expected of him. Unknown to anyone, Papa had actually been watching the masquerade party from a corner of his eye right from when it entered his street.

As if from nowhere, Papa suddenly thundered from upstairs and ordered the fellows to be gone immediately, otherwise fire would descend on their heads. In a jiffy the entire party fled! Not the Igunnu itself, nor its outriders remained behind. An Alhaji neighbour of Papa's who had watched the entire scenario with interest, commented loudly after the masquerades, *"don't you fellows k now who lives on this street?"* *"You certainly mad e the greatest mistake of your lives, missing your way to this area!"* All the years that Papa lived on that street no masquerades passed by nor moved near the area.

COUNCIL PEOPLE:
AN EYE-WITNESS ACCOUNT

There was a time that Lagos State Council officials came to Papa's church. They alleged that the church walls had extended beyond the permitted bounds. They were there to pull down the walls. Papa's attention was called and he came out of his office to see the Council people. *"What is the matter sirs?"* They told him they were there to pull down the church walls because it was in the right of way. Papa replied, *"Oh, I see."* *"But what were you told?"* *"Whose house did they tell you this is, my house?"* The council officials answered Papa that they were told the place was a church. That meant it was the house of God. Papa then said to them, *"Good."* *"Since you have been told Who has the house, go ahead then and pull it down. It is not my house."*

No, 9 Willoughby Street, the little front shop where it all started

The present RCCG headquarters building constructed on the original site
of the first (all planks) church building
(formerly 1, Cemetery street), now Redemption Way, Ebute- Metta

Pastor Rathod receiving his ordination certificate from Papa Akindayomi

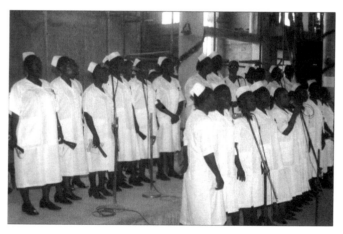

RCCG nurses, midwives & matrons during a public presentation

Papa posing in front of his first (all planks) church building

Fresh graduates of the Redeemed Bible College (Pst. Mulero in bow tie). With them is Pastor Rathod (a Canadian ordained by Rev. Akindayomi)

Ordination day: newly ordained pastors with Papa in 1975.
Far right is young Pastor Adejare Adeboye

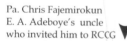

Rev. J. O. Akindayomi with
his protégé, E. A. Adeboye

Pa. Chris Fajemirokun
E. A. Adeboye's uncle
who invited him to RCCG

Inside the first RCCG church building
(*Notice the hand fan on the side stool-no electric fans!*)

Papa's first daughter's wedding party pose in front of the church at Ebute Metta

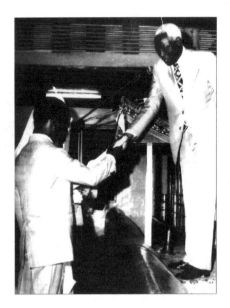

Papa congratulating a newly wedded couple in the church

Newly wedded couple receiving their marriage
certificate from the church secretary, Rev. Olonade

Papa preaching with his interpreter on Thanksgiving Day

25years down the road: *"Father we thank You for Your faithfulness."*
Today dancing is permitted!

Thanksgiving Sunday during RCCG 25th anniversary in 1977

God has been good... Papa leading the church in thanksgiving

With that he turned and walked briskly away from the Council officials. Much perplexed the men had no idea what to do next. Not daring to touch the walls they soon left and never came back.

A MAN OF INTEGRITY

Within his area of influence Papa had a reputation for being a man of God from the heart. People from far and wide trusted him and had a high regard for his opinion. The majority of his church members at this early period were not highly educated people. The most prominent member of the Ebute-Metta congregation then was said to be a certain Awobajo who was a Manager with G. B. Ollivant. There was a Sanitary Superintendent (*Wolewole*) with the Lagos Mainland Council and the others in the congregation were just this and that. But Papa's stand on probity was so well known beyond his church walls that whenever Kingsway Stores or Leventis or other such companies needed cashiers they contacted Rev. Akindayomi to please send prospective candidates to them from among his people. And if Papa sent you to any of these places you had an instant employment. They would not bother to interview you again.

That Papa sent you meant you were of a very high level of responsibility and trust. Hardly did these big companies ever regret any employee they took by Papa's recommendation. Such was the level of trust in Papa's integrity and fear of God.

Papa's nephew Ebenezer Olufemi Ademulegun came to

Lagos in search of a job and eventually joined the Nigerian Police Force. Members of his unit used to be assigned as security detail to big banks. Eventually he ended up with the Central Bank of Nigeria (CBN) in 1977 and was assigned to Control Room (Movement Division). His monthly salary was N2:00 (two naira). Following this development Papa called Ebenezer and said to him, "*my son, don't forget in that place that you are a child of God. You must make your stand very clear and well known.*" In other words, do not compromise your Christian identity.

Any bank naturally was a place of temptation for a young man as far as money was concerned, and especially with such poor pay. Anyway young Ademulegun kept his uncle's admonition close to his heart and never forgot it. He knew that Papa hardly spoke to you if there was no reason for it. Not too long afterwards a situation arose which tested the young man's grit. In Movement (*i.e carrying of money from and to different locations*) , the operational law was that any money moved any time after 6:00p.m. was at the owner's risk. Not the security detail nor any bank official was liable if anything went wrong. Safe law, don't you think? Ademulegun in company of the bank officials one day went to evacuate a large amount from Maiduguri in the far north to Lagos.

By the time they were airborne it was close to 8:00p.m. In the aircraft Ademulegun suddenly noticed that the box of money had cut in half! Apparently he was not the only observant person, but his colleagues rather invited him along that they help themselves to some free cash. He bluntly refused. Papa's admonition was burning in his heart like fire. The bank inspector came back again trying to persuade him, but he told the man, *"Please count me out!"* Ademulegun kept a close watch on the box by placing his foot on it throughout their flight, maintaining a straight face. On arrival in Lagos he personally audited the money and then submitted the papers.

Before now United Bank for Africa (UBA) had offered him appointment twice but each time he tried to leave Papa told him, *"no, not yet. Wait."* In his own words Ademulegun recalled: *"And you know if you follow whatever Papa says it always leads to peace and joy."* Thus he had stayed back. However one year after the Maiduguri episode UBA invited him again, and this time Papa told him: *"Go, because now the glory of God will be manifested on your behalf."* And so he left the CBN in 1979. Exactly one week after Ademulegun's departure, some misdemeanour was uncovered at the Control Room and the police was called in. During investigations one of the Managers who knew Ademulegun personally asked after him and was told: *"Ademulegun is no more here."* The man's instant response was *"no wonder!"*

Eventually all of Ademulegun's former colleagues at the Control Room ended with the Force CID, Alagbon. The people spent no less than one calendar year cooling their heels in detention. Why did the young man have a testimony in that kind of place? He answers the question himself: "*it was because of Papa's admonition and counsel. The fear of his displeasure could never permit me to join evil company.*"

Another one of Papa's nephews who also lived with him, Olawole Ogunsakin, concurred that his uncle was truly loving but in his words, "*Papa was very disciplined and tolerated no nonsense from any child.*" Ogunsakin recalled how shortly after his National Youth Service in the North he had grown a quite bushy beard, just to appear fashionable like other young men his age. He was planning for his marriage and came home to inform Papa. On his arrival Papa looked his nephew up and down and asked: "*what is the meaning of that?,*" pointing at his large beard. Papa said he wanted to know what the young man was doing with the thing. Right there Papa sent for shaving stick and personally shaved off Olawole's mark of pride. Afterwards he asked, "*yes, how much did you say the soft drinks for your wedding reception would cost?*" Olawole told him, and Papa counted the complete money right there and gave to his nephew, with the comment that, "*now you look responsible enough for me to follow you to go ask for your bride!*" Of course the young man could only say "yes sir" and fall in line.

AN APOSTOLIC MENTOR
Papa had a stature in the Spirit that anyone watching his dealings with the high and low could not doubt. Despite being uneducated, his grasp and deep understanding of spiritual principles were legendary. And Papa would

take personal interest in anyone who seemed to have a heart for God, gladly and willingly sharing with them his deep insight into spiritual reality. Papa would also willingly make any personal sacrifices necessary to establish such a person on a firm footing.

One day a certain young man *(who had been long coming in the spirit)* arrived Papa's church and an eternal spiritual bonding was established between them instantly. For no less than five years now Papa Akindayomi had mentioned it repeatedly to his church that his successor was not yet in their midst. However he constantly gave them the person's complete description: height, build, jacket size, et. al. What he didn't know was the person's name and location. Every once in a while, both in church and at home Papa sang that song in his people's ears.

One glorious Sunday morning, the expected visitor came to church and Papa recognised him on the instant. He wasted no time making his acquaintance and striking up a father-son relationship with the young man who never knew what lay ahead for him. As a matter of fact Papa personally assigned the job of visitation to himself on this day. And he visited the new comer immediately after morning service.

A university scholar, very polished and much exposed suddenly found himself the pupil of a barely literate church man whose authority with God seriously challenged his own intellectual prowess. Papa took to him like a duck to water. Unto him this son indeed had been given. The man used to be addressed as Dr. (Enoch Adejare) Adeboye, a mathematics lecturer at the University of Lagos. But by the time he and Papa had gone a certain number of years together, he eventually became known as Pastor (Enoch Adejare) Adeboye and had become Papa's interpreter. Papa rapidly graduated him into the Elders' Fellowship and gave him the appellation of *"young elder"* because his natural age did not yet qualify him for that Group.

When Papa Josiah Olufemi Akindayomi was ready to go home finally some seven years later, his spiritual mantle had fallen clearly on this inseparable disciple and beloved son. Adeboye initially thought it was a huge joke, but Papa knew it was a solemn declaration, when on their first acquaintance he had told the young man that he was stepping into his shoes after transition. God had decreed it so even before his arrival.

Rev. Akindayomi's apostolic ministry was not confined to the walls of his own church alone but went beyond. There was a time he got to hear the story of another young lecturer who was doing a great work for the Lord on the University (of Lagos) campus. Papa was told that the Lord was blessing the work *(comprised mainly of Bible Studies and Prayer)* but the fellowship leader was having problems with the University authorities. The name of the budding man of God was a certain William F. Kumuyi.

He had started the fellowship in the sitting room of his official quarters on campus. His unusual brilliance as a Mathematics teacher used to bring very many young people under his influence, who would not escape without having the gospel presented to them. Therefore his brilliant academic endowment acted as a divine hook with which the Lord was bringing many lost souls back home. His ministry expanded quickly and soon his teeming crowd attracted the attention of university authorities who cared less for such religious stuff. They began to give the man problems such that the prospects of Kumuyi's teaching career were being seriously threatened.

God positioned Papa Akindayomi strategically at this critical period as a pillar of strength and encouragement to Pastor Kumuyi and his young ministry. Thus when Papa heard of the travails of the young man of God he got so interested that he sent for him. The year was 1974. When W. F. Kumuyi answered Papa's call, he was taken in as a son just like young (Pastor) Adeboye. Papa scheduled special times every week when he had personal Bible studies, prayer and deep sharing in the secrets of walking with God, with these promising young men. He challenged them, encouraged them, admonished them, and in some certain areas corrected their doctrines. Papa's depth of the scriptures used to daze the two brilliant academicians.

Research revealed that Papa encouraged Kumuyi to adjust the nomenclature of his fellowship from Deeper

Life Ministry to include church. Papa based his advice on the book of Revelation where John addressed his letters to different churches of Christ. Papa pointed out to Pastor Kumuyi also that in Apostle Paul's letter to the Romans he asked to greet the church at Priscilla and Aquila's house, not ministry. Ministry may be an organisation, but church is about people. In good faith Pastor Kumuyi accepted Papa's correction and thus started the church arm of his Deeper Christian Life Ministry called Deeper Life Bible Church. Papa also made his church and all the facilities available to Pastor Kumuyi and his teeming crowd. As a result their weekly Bible Study was moved out of campus to RCCG facilities, at Ebute Metta with Papa's full blessing. This ended Pastor Kumuyi's headache with accommodation for his meetings.

Another area which particularly gave Papa concern in the Deeper Life teachings, had to do with marriage. It seemed not to be an important or even necessary issue with the group. As a result, the need for marriage was somehow downplayed. It was as if marriage violated their understanding of the doctrine of holiness. This gave Papa Akindayomi great concern, especially as he noticed young men and women passing the flower of their youth, and yet remaining unmarried without being bothered about it. Papa courageously stepped into this dicey area too and in the light of Scriptures along with the help of the Holy Spirit convinced Pastor Kumuyi that marriage was good, honourable and actually not a sin even for committed Christians.

As a matter of fact, not marrying was an easier route into sin and temptation than marrying. Pastor Kumuyi himself at this time was still single and he was not young for marriage. A very humble, teachable and eager learner, the budding pastor submitted to Papa Akindayomi in this area of his doctrinal understanding also. It was to everybody's joy and happiness when brother W. F. Kumuyi and Sister Biodun, one of the founding members of his fellowship became joined in holy matrimony sometime later. This encouraged and reassured others in the Deeper Life that marriage was ordained of God and should not be despised nor disregarded in the name of spirituality. Pastor W. F. Kumuyi's marriage was eventually blessed with two sons.

Papa kept his interest alive in all that had to do with W. F. Kumuyi even though Kumuyi was not under his own ministry. When the Deeper Life Bible Church finally secured their own site at Gbagada, which had to be reclaimed from water as Papa's site at Ebute-Metta was, everything that needed to be done to put the place in shape was provided by Papa and his people. When Kumuyi's International Bible Training Centre (IBTC), at Ayobo-Ipaja was to take off several years later, Papa was invited to perform the foundation laying ceremony.

Today Pastor W. F. Kumuyi, who has the third largest single congregation in the world; is a major pride to the nation of Nigeria, as his stature and record have been such that he is respected even beyond our shores. Thanks to the faithfulness and large-heartedness of the man of God, J. O. Akindayomi, a soldier of the cross.

HOLINESS AND PRAYER LIFE

Papa's utter hatred for sin was renowned. The very appearance of ungodliness did not escape his eagle eye and he punctured it instantly. You did not stay long around Papa to know that he was a man of God's presence. Morning, afternoon, evening, throughout the night, Papa was praying consciously or unconsciously in his spirit. He hardly had a time he was not talking to God about something and he prayed about everything. Even mundane things as a wristwatch or shoe, Papa would tell you to pray about it, because God is a faithful God.

Present General Overseer, E. A. Adeboye is believed to have directly inherited Papa's passion for holiness in body and spirit. For Papa, holiness was a lifestyle, and never a doctrine. You must live holy if you would ever be pleasing in God's sight. Holiness meant avoiding every appearance of anything that is questionable or not straight forward. In the natural, Papa passionately hated anything unclean. His physical appearance reflected a sparkling personality. He noticed everything. Even a speck of dust! Thus shoddiness could never survive around him. You could never work with Papa and be sloppy or appear shabbily.

Papa loved colour white. Thus he insisted that his driver's uniform be a set of white suit complete with cap. On the crest of the cap rested the RCCG logo. Himself loved coming out dapper. Except you were told, Papa's dressing could never reveal to you that he never went to school. On top of his clean cut suit, neat tie and sparkling shoes, Papa loved to wear a bowler hat. A number of his close aides claimed that Papa it was who taught them how to knot their ties. Apart from his faithful bowler hat, he loved wearing suspenders too. When Papa walked up to you he cut the picture of a university professor about to deliver one of those great inaugural lectures! And his dressing was not complete without his wristwatch. If Papa wore native dress, which he loved to keep very simple, it was with the same attention to detail. He loved quality goods.

These seemingly mundane things revealed a heart that had touched a depth of excellence in God. Nothing could be done anyhow around Papa. When serving his food, you had to take care to see that all dishes and utensils were spotless. Papa washed his hands with white Lux soap after eating. His napkin was a white tea towel. All his things must be kept clean and neat. His private sitting room was personally decorated by him. He strategically placed flowers, photos, and mementoes all around.

Despite being intolerant of sin or misbehaviour, Papa hardly uttered angry words. As he advanced in his walk with God it became increasingly difficult for him to get angry with people. Even when provoked or challenged he kept quiet, rather than say anything out of provocation. Once a fellow Ondo man challenged Papa to a duel of words, but he replied the man, *"Sorry, I am no longer an Ondo man, I am now a citizen of the Kingdom of God."* And with that he walked away from the man. The natural Akindayomi would dress you down to your pants! But not this regenerated man of God.

He was much an indoors man and in the early days of the ministry communicated little with the household. Domestic affairs were left strictly to Mama. Papa spent much time in meditation, Bible studies, and in praying for those that sought his prayer ministry.

The awesome presence on Papa was so palpable that people did not approach him anyhow, even members of his own household. All who lived or worked with him confessed that surely Papa was someone you could never lie to successfully. Even when you had planned your story ahead and rehearsed it on your way, when you got into Papa's presence you told him nothing but the truth. Papa would tell his people that it's the work of the Holy Spirit to reveal the truth. And reveal it He did! It was always a difficult exercise attempting to deceive the man in any way. A forceful hook elicited the true story from your mouth.

A FUNNY EPISODE

Once upon a time, Papa's son, Pastor E. A. Adeboye had travelled from his present Ilorin base to see Papa in Lagos. Probably he forgot to buy something along the way for the old man as his manner was. But when he arrived Yaba on his way to Papa's house at 6, Kufeji Street, behind the Casino at Rowe Park, Pastor Adeboye bought oranges to present to Papa. On arrival he presented the oranges as if he had bought them on his journey from Ilorin. Papa accepted the oranges and thanked his son, then asked suddenly, *"did you say you bought them on your way from Ilorin?,"* the man promptly said, *"Yes sir!"*

Soon it was time to go and the younger man got up to go, but hardly had he stepped out of Papa's presence when the Spirit of God began to trouble him that he had actually told a lie to the old man. Quickly he turned back to Papa and asked, *"Sir, were you asking about those oranges I just brought for you?"* Papa said, *"Yes my son."* *"You wanted to know if I bought them on my way from Ilorin. Papa, actually I bought them at Yaba before I got here!"* Papa was happy with his son, and he promptly exclaimed, *"Thank God for the Holy Spirit!"* Papa Akindayomi was never known by his many sons in the faith to be forceful. Rather he was loving, caring but very firm. He would never bend the rules for anyone, no matter how much he loves you. But they all confess that if you were humble enough and patient to follow Papa's teachings and you were obedient to his admonitions you would see yourself prospering and doing so well in life.

HE SAW HEAVEN!
It had started as a mere cold and some little cough. His whole body suddenly felt tired and weak. Obviously the fatigue of daily ministry was taking its toll. Papa decided to go to Ibadan to have a little rest. This was early 1980. However, he had spent only one or two days in Ibadan

and God instructed him to return to Lagos. Promptly, he came back. But somehow, the weakness would not leave his body. Rather than improve, he got progressively weaker. Well, why not? After all, he had finally ordained a white man, as God had promised him, that that would be his last major assignment. Maybe it was time to go.

Papa was well ready to go home. Around September when he would not amend, a round-the-clock prayer chain was organised at his house by the church to keep watch on the beloved man of God. After a few days, Papa had a complaint about the prayer warriors-they were disturbing his spirit! Their prayers were preventing him from concentrating, it's as if God wanted to tell him something. He therefore said he did not want them near his bedroom anymore. They should move to the farthest part of the house. And they complied. By the middle of the month of October, Papa passed on. He was all alone in his room when that happened. Not knowing for how long he had been in that state, Mama Egbedire it was who found Papa in this condition.

In the words of Pastor J. A. O. Akindele, a foundation member and an eye-witness of these things; "we had started to sing "ile lo lo tarara,"' (although no medical personnel was called in to certify Papa dead). In Yoruba land, when an old person dies, they sing "ile lo lo tarara," meaning the dead person has gone straight home. Papa was in that death state for some days. His body was not completely cold but a little warm and somehow lifeless.

Yes, Papa went home but the journey was not so smooth. He got to heaven but was not permitted in. He was even given a glimpse of his own home! Yet he was stopped short, and ordered back to earth. Why?

On coming back, Papa related to his wife what strange encounter he had had. God revisited with him a matter of 24 years before, and asked him to go make the necessary amends.

What could that be? Everybody was shocked: it was the burning of his tracts by the Apostolic Faith Church way back in 1956! What? Papa related in accurate details to Mama what happened, the summary of which was that he must go back to make up and make peace with Brother T. He was to forgive the man for burning his tracts back in 1956! Despite Papa's passionate pleas that he be allowed to stay, no such thing was granted him. Even when Papa complained with feeling that Brother T. should not have burnt those tracts; yet heaven insisted that he still must go back to forgive Brother T. And so Rev. Akindayomi was sent back to earth to make peace with his fellow brother.

Rev. Akindayomi had had no qualms about names, thus his reason for changing his own Ogo Oluwa Prayer Society to Apostolic Church of Africa. He had much love for the teachings of the Apostolic Faith Church, and in his own simple belief, the Church of Christ was one. He didn't understand why people should have to fight over what name a church bore. But apart from this, unconfirmed reports also alleged that letters began to get mixed up between the Apostolic Faith Church Lagos, and the Apostolic Church of Africa, because both were in the same vicinity.

However, now that God had corrected him, he was willing and ready to let go of his own position of defence and apologise. Moreover when the angels that turned him back showed Papa countless preachers, some still with their collars on, chained down or rejected from God's presence for one unconfessed sin or unresolved matter or the other, yet he was given a second chance of grace, Papa needed no long persuasion. When he came back to life Papa called his own people together to share this unique experience with them.

Afterwards, he reported himself at the Apostolic Faith headquarters. Papa related his experience, apologised to the leadership and made every necessary amend, including a personal letter of forgiveness to Bro. T for the 1952 incident; asking the man's own forgiveness as well.

This repentant attitude affected the Apostolic Faith Church leadership so much that they developed a closer tie with Papa and his church. When Papa finally went to be with the Lord, Apostolic Faith Church was fully represented at his funeral. Pastor Oshokoya personally attested to the fact that Rev. Akindayomi was indeed a true man of God, and surely he had gone to be with the Lord. Brother T. himself went to be with the Lord exactly three years after, on November 16, 1983.

One other effect of this experience on Papa was that he began to admonish his people to start asking God to show them their own home in heaven, so that they could be free of the love of the world and everything in it. He said it would also help them to live their lives as if each day they had was their last.

NOTES
1. Term Paper (titled "Independent Churches and Cults") submitted to Theological College of Northern Nigeria, Bukuru. Plateau State: P. 1
2. Roberts Liardon: **John G. Lake, The Complete Collection of His Life Teachings** . Albury Publishing Tulsa, Ok., 1999: 415

CHAPTER FIVE

THE WALK OF FAITH

WHEN PROPHET JOSIAH ARRIVED Lagos in 1941 accompanied by his young wife, he had nothing else but God as his sole possession. He had seen God variously at work in his life over the years, therefore he had great faith in his heart that God would not disappoint him now.

THE GOD OF COVENANT

Don't forget that God had told him way back in Ile-Ife that he was not to be a salaried servant of God. God had said to him categorically, *"I shall be your Source..."* One thing about Rev. Akindayomi was that he had such childlike faith in God, that whatever God told him he believed implicitly and walked in it without flinching.

Since God had said *"no salary"* he had adjusted his life and mind accordingly and adopted a lifestyle of faith that became his covenant agreement with God. He was devoted to serving the Lord full-time, choosing to survive any way he could while waiting upon the Lord's mercy. However that's better said than experienced. In point of fact, Papa's wife, Esther Egbedire it was who had to shoulder the bulk of domestic responsibilities at this critical waiting period while Papa locked himself away with God. According to Papa himself: *"When we arrived Lagos we had no food supply from anywhere. Therefore I used to go to church to pray daily from 9:00 a.m. to 4:00 p.m. My wife would go out to do load-carrier. Sometimes she would come back home with one shilling. This she would use to prepare a meal for the two of us. At this period we ate only once a day, and that lasted for complete one year. However we were happy and never despaired."* [1] Prophet Josiah's grace and gift eventually began to make way for him and things improved somewhat.

However it was soon time to separate from the C&S in obedience to God's directions. The following was Papa's comments about the aftermath of that action: *"The flow of people that used to throng me for prayer and also bless me materially ceased. Things became so bad again that feeding became a big issue once more."* [2] So what did the man of God do? *"Satan engineered that so that I could go back. But the Lord strengthened me to resolve that whatsoever may come, even death, I would never go back to the C&S. Consequently I sold my bed, cupboard, prayer dress (white garment), and all my big agbada in order to start this church."* [3] Things didn't improve immediately nor did miracles start to happen on the instant. Rather Papa said: *"I started going to our meeting place (at 9, Willoughby Street) to pray accompanied with fasting for a total of six months."* [4]

All this while Papa interacted very little with his immediate family, because he was always in God's presence, fasting, praying and meditating. Whenever he came out it was almost impossible to look at his face. His eyes were as a pure river of glory, it was as if God looked through them into people's very souls. Papa spent much time studying at the feet of the Holy Spirit, who in the words of Kathryn Khulman is *"the greatest Teacher in the world."* On Fridays he did not come out at all. Having understood the kind of call upon her husband's life Mama Egbedire never complained. With time she was able to switch from load carrying to wholesale firewood business, and later on added petty household provision to her trading.

Papa's children had their own share of the afflictions of the Gospel because, while growing they would hawk bread in the morning before going to school and in the evening when they come back, to further subsidise the family income. *"Good food,"* in the words of Pastor (Mrs.) Akindele, *"was a rare luxury at home at this time."* The hard days of sowing in tears took years, but soon an incredible teaching anointing began to manifest in Rev. Akindayomi's life and it was obvious to all. Despite his lack of formal education, Papa's wisdom and grasp of the Scriptures were phenomenal. His own very presence was awesome and commanded much reverence.

When more and more people had begun to seek him for

different needs, Papa did not forget God's command that he was not to take a salary. Thus even gifts from people he had prayed for were scrupulously screened. He didn't take gifts easily. After he had left the C&S and began to pay extra attention to the Word of God, Papa became more meticulous with everything that has to do with walking with God. The more he delved into the Scriptures the more he discovered the core of the heart of God, and the more he conformed himself to God's will, thereby accurately positioning himself as a man after God's heart.

God also decided to make things easy for His servant in the place of ministry. He didn't struggle to pray for people, command situations to turn around, or prophesy particularly into people's lives. If Papa gave you a word from the Lord it was 100% accurate.

THE ETERNAL FOUNDATION: FAITHFULNESS

When God insisted to father Abraham that he give gifts to all other children and let them go, but retain only Isaac in the house it sounded like a harsh judgment. But God's foolishness is even wiser than our own wisdom. God's own wisdom is never questionable. He had told Abraham that Isaac was the son of His covenant with him, and therefore only Isaac was to stay back and get the inheritance.

Likewise it appeared quite "unwise" when Papa Akindayomi would not affiliate with foreign missions as the few existing independent ministries at that early time were doing. Papa claimed that God said he was not to affiliate his church with any foreign mission, even though part of God's promises to him was that RCCG would spread all over the world.

Joining up was a "good" idea because it meant the local church had a more respectable profile, got covering from the foreign mission, and received financial and material support as well. But Papa Akindayomi abstained, especially since the alliance with G. Lake's ministry ended the way it did. Why wouldn't he grab such a golden opportunity? It's obvious he was seriously anointed. But the man says God said "no." Many rushed at these offers with speed, because it was obviously a much cheaper and faster way of gaining prominence. According to Papa's first son, Pastor Kolade Akindayomi, what Papa said was that it would be difficult eventually to know what God did and what was of men if he took up the foreign offers. On the basis of this, all other offers that came were rejected.

This is quite a lesson in the walk of faith by Rev. J. O. Akindayomi. He was undoubtedly a man of deep faith in God. Remember the Word of God that says: **"That ye be not slothful, but followers of them who through faith and patience inherit the promises"** (Hebrews 6:12). The Bible says it was only after father Abraham had patiently endured that he inherited the promise of God. The story of Rev. J. O. Akindayomi was no different. His patience revealed the depth of his faith in God, Whose

Word alone is our evidence of things not yet seen.

The promise of God is always a release of Himself to a mere mortal, and this often manifests in the stability of the heritage of such a person. You will notice that king Saul lost out with God because he was always cutting corners with God's instruction. Therefore after his demise we saw that **"...the house of Saul grew weaker and weaker"** (2 Samuel 3:1). You may wonder why? It was because God did not intend to retain Saul's legacy in Israel. Therefore his posterity was allowed to fizzle out. However you will notice that when father Abraham had patiently waited upon all the covenant demands and testing from God, God finally said unto him, **"I will never leave you nor forsake you,"** and beloved, we are witnesses that God never forsook Abraham nor his seed till today.

As a matter of fact you and I are of the seed of Abraham. The seed in the ground of the house of Abraham to which we all belong is his unflinching faith in God. That was the faith that brought forth Isaac. Abraham had to do everything God demanded before Isaac could be released unto him.

Therefore you must begin to understand what the implications would be, when God chose a narrow path and commanded His servant to walk straitly in it, not veering to the right nor to the left. That meant coming generations of Akindayomi's spiritual seed would always experience the covenant benefits of that relationship.

Their father had walked with God by covenant, and he never broke faith with the Lord. It was a covenant of obedience.

This should begin to give you an insight also into the phenomenal influence, spread and wealth of the Redeemed Christian Church of God as it is today. Their root goes way down into the ground of faith in the covenant-keeping God. Papa Akindayomi had been promised by God that if he would keep his church free of questionable fund-raising methods *(such as harvest, bazaar, etc)*, like other churches around him then, that He God would prosper his church so much that their wealth would stagger the imagination of onlookers and raise eyebrows.

The Holy Spirit alone was to be given prime place in the church's affairs. Papa chose to keep faith with God in this regard also. God kept His word! Even though the church could still be considered as being at its infancy in Papa's days, but God gave him a chauffeur-driven Benz 280 automatic, among some other vehicles, and certain categories of church officers also had official cars with drivers. For an un-affiliated indigenous church in Nigeria of that period, that was a lot of clout. Today, even a casual observer will readily concede that the Redeemed Church is a prosperous church. The calibre of its membership says a lot for its influence and strength. Moreover its choice properties and well-appointed worship centres within the shores of Nigeria and beyond testify to the goodness of God in the life of this church.

"I WILL BUILD MY CHURCH"

Papa was equally commanded by God to follow the Holy Spirit strictly in structuring his church administration. He was to allow the Lord to influence his choice of persons into key positions, and never rely on his own feelings. When the issue of succession arose, Papa's taking this initial advice from God proved a tremendous help. Perhaps RCCG would have been like some other churches by now, which after the founder's demise not only split, but had different factions ending up in different hands with diverse teachings and practices. RCCG remained one and intact, because the founder realised that the Church belonged to the Lord and only He could build it, not any man. He never did his own thing but relied completely on the administration of the Holy Spirit (see I Corinthians 12: 4-6).

When men build by themselves, the proper appellation for it is personal empire not church. By deliberate policy Papa Akindayomi never created the post or office of Assistant Superintendent. This proved a decision of accurate wisdom, when eventually the issue of actual succession arose. There was no next-in-command to contend with, since he never had an official Assistant in that sense of the word.

All close associates and leaders were unequivocally impressed with the fact that none of them was a *"second-in-command"* or so-called *"Crown Prince"* to the man of God. The Lord had said his successor was coming and he would be nothing near the present crop of leadership.

And you know anything God told him, Papa would tell his people. The whole church workers heard it for years on end that Papa's successor would be a new comer. Papa constantly told the church workers to pray fervently to God to send the person. And of course God did not disappoint His servant. Faith+Patience paid very high dividends for Papa Akindayomi, and his transition never led to any form of chaos in the house he had laboured so diligently to build. The Almighty God saw to that. The day Adeboye arrived Papa said to the church workers: *"You can stop praying about the new leader now. God has brought him."*

As it happened during the transition period in Israel, that even though David was waiting in the wings by God's appointment, a few other men also had the ambition of ascending that same throne. The unseen hands of the Almighty cleared the scene in very interesting ways (see 2 Samuel 2-4).

A few hopefuls around Rev. Akindayomi who could see the way the cookie was trying to crumble after the arrival of *"the leader of tomorrow,"* (E.A. Adeboye), either fell out with the old man or left in anger somewhere along the line. Papa never personally cursed or sent anyone away.

"THIS IS MY BELOVED SON... HEAR HIM"
From his first visit to the little church at the lagoon front, his life never remained the same again. The man had come to this church in desperation when it appeared that the life of his beloved wife might be in danger. They

had had three children-all by Caesarean sectioning. And doctors had advised that they put a stop to child bearing. They thought they were keeping the doctor's advice, when somehow a fourth pregnancy showed up. Tension arose in the hearts of both husband and wife. Coupled with that, their last child became afflicted with a strange disease. Push came to shove, especially when the couple had exhausted the rounds of orthodox, traditional as well as spiritual practitioners. Nothing availed.

This fine scholar became desperate enough to seek help wherever he could find it. His uncle, Rev. Chris Fajemirokun, an elder in the church, suggested the Redeemed Christian Church of God. It was a little church, and the whole environment was rather humble and lowly but God's presence was there. The man of God in the place was a thorough prophet and his prayers were razor-sharp. The younger man agreed to be persuaded, because he just must get a solution somehow. And so he walked into an ancient door that God had kept open for him even before he was born, a door of destiny. When he came, God was waiting for him, and straight into His everlasting arms did he land!

Dr. E. A. Adeboye, Mathematics lecturer at the University of Lagos and with the ultimate ambition of becoming the youngest Vice-Chancellor in Africa ran his tall ambition into God's incinerator that day he walked into the funny little church at the lagoon front. God began to pursue him afterwards.

Since the memorable day in July (29) 1973, when he finally surrendered his life to Christ until the dying minutes of 1980 when the white-headed old man passed away into glory, he never left Adeboye alone. The young man would rather pursue his academic career, fulfill his personal dream and also serve the Lord as best he could, but Papa Akindayomi felt otherwise. Rather he wanted his son in the Lord *(whom God had promised him for very many years before he finally arrived)*, to yield to God's plan for his life and shelve his own dreams. God wanted him to step into the leader's shoes after transition. To Adeboye that was the hugest of jokes he had heard in his life, except that Akindayomi wasn't a man given to joking or any form of frivolity. He told Adeboye that taking over leadership of RCCG after the present leader's demise, was God's definite plan for him.

"THE LEADER OF TOMORROW"
There were much more older men around, yes, as old as his own father perhaps; but God had chosen him. Adeboye and his wife, Folu, went into frantic prayers, desiring God to please change His mind, but God is not a man-He neither lies nor alters His mind. He had decided long before Adeboye was even born again. Interestingly the sick child that had even brought them to Redeemed church had eventually died! But the One they were facing now was the Almighty God Himself, and they found no way of escaping His long arms.

Papa went everywhere proudly with his son the *"leader of tomorrow"* that God had promised him. Anywhere he would preach, *"young elder"* Adeboye was his interpreter. Apart from the long hours of private sessions with Adeboye in his bedroom, Papa also gave his son assignments to prepare sermons, which he would read to him and have him correct. He began to imbibe so much of Papa Akindayomi's spirit and lifestyle. It was no secret that Adeboye had his own personal room in Papa Akindayomi's home, because often they were together into the wee hours of the next morning. Whatever they were discussing only heaven was witness of it, because not even Mama Egbedire was invited to any of their private sessions. Many nights after keeping an endless vigil over their dinner, Mama would go to bed, and wake up in the morning to meet her food in exactly the same position as she had placed it the night before! Papa had many things to tell his son and show him, and time was very short. And Adeboye was such an eager learner. They also had quite interesting experiences together.

One day Papa wanted Pastor Adeboye and some other young pastors around to load a large refrigerator unto the back seat of a car. Try as hard they could the thing would just not enter. The men laboured hard but the fridge was adamant. All the while Papa watched with keen interest. When the young men sweating profusely became tired, Papa came closer and told them, *"turn this way, and push the thing in that way."* They hardly believed it. In a few minutes the task was completed and the fridge entered the same space they had thought was too small for it.

Adeboye learned and saw Papa Akindayomi teaching

and living and practising faith first hand. To the old man anything under the heavens was possible, especially when you've spoken to God about it. Did he pray about the fridge? Only God knows!

"BEHOLD I GIVE UNTO YOU..."

In July of 1977 Papa went on pilgrimage to Israel with Pastor Igbekoyi, one of his assistant pastors. On the Israel journey the plane made a stop at Rome and Papa was privileged to meet the reigning Pope with whom he had an audience. While in Israel God said to the man of God, *"start tidying things up, Dr. E. A. Adeboye, the leader of tomorrow will be taking over soon ..."* [5], this was the same year Adeboye was ordained a pastor. Papa took God's admonition very seriously, drawing Adeboye closer than ever before with specific instructions and words of counsel.

In 1979, Papa travelled together with Adeboye to America, to attend Kenneth Hagin's Camp Meeting, and he made up his mind on that trip to pour his all finally into the new vessel. Thus Papa enjoined those with him that day to join him in praying for Pastor Adeboye as his definitive successor. In the words of Pastor E. A. Adeboye himself this was what happened that day: *"we were in the hotel and Papa was leading prayers. As the intensity of prayers increased the hotel building began to shake to its foundation. Soon the hotel staff knocked at our door demanding to know what heavy equipment we were using that was causing the observed tremor because they had identified our room as the source of the tremor. So we opened the door for them explaining that we were not using any heavy equipment.*" [6] It was a once in a lifetime kind of prayer and a never to be forgotten day.

It took another year before the transfer of mantle took place in the physical, but already it was accomplished in the Spirit and Papa was satisfied.

NOTES

1) Rev. J. O. Akindayomi's memoirs
2) Ibid.,
3) Ibid.,
4) Ibid.,
5) Olusola, Ajayi (Dr.) DVM, **Warrior of Righteousness: The Life and Ministry of Rev. J.O. Akindayomi** (Abeokuta, Nigeria: Ordinance Publishing House, 1997), 84
6) Ibid., 74

CHAPTER SIX

EYE-WITNESS ACCOUNTS

My Life with Papa Akindayomi
FROM DRIVER TO PASTOR:
Z. A. Mulero *(Papa's driver from 1973-80)*

I FIRST MET PAPA IN 1969 AT ITAMAYA, Ibadan when he came on pastoral visit to our church. This was the first RCCG Parish in Ibadan.

My first impression of Papa Akindayomi was that of a holy man, a man of God. There was a certain aura of glory about him, which made him look like an angel. He cut the picture of a sinless person. He was solemn. His entire head was covered with snow white hair.

THE AKINDAYOMI I KNEW
I had started as a driver to one of the elders of the church, Rev. Akinlembola, a very close associate of Papa; but through divinely arranged circumstances I became

Papa's personal driver in 1973 and I was moved from Ibadan to Lagos. I began to live with Papa officially, at his residence at 6, Kufeji street, Yaba in the year 1974, and I was about 26 years old.

Papa's life was a very unique one. He was a man of much prayer and he used to fast a lot. It's as if he doesn't sleep. I used to feel that probably he went to heaven at night and came back to earth in the morning. The first time I was invited into his presence it occurred to me instinctively that to work and live with this man would be quite a herculean task! I had work to do on myself. He had such a commanding personality. He abhors shoddiness of any sort and he notices everything. Papa was a very expressive person. If he was angry or happy with you he made it known in clear terms. As a result of working and living with him, so many areas of my own life-spiritual, and personal, including my appearance were radically affected. He made me to become meticulous with everything.

A MAN OF SPEED!
Papa's car was Benz 280 automatic, and he loved for us to cruise with it! He hated slow driving with a passion. My secret appellation for Papa was *"Road Made for Speed."* If I drove under 120km.p.h on a journey, Papa would be rather dissatisfied and he would complain. He used to tell me, *"my son, I know I can't die by road accident. So don't be afraid. Just move!"* With this I would accordingly increase my speed and coast on. Sometimes as we were travelling Papa may suddenly ask me, *"Mulero, is*

anything wrong with your car today?" If my answer was no, Papa would say *"then speed it up, man. Move!"* Between Lagos and Ibadan it would take us only forty(40)minutes, and on arrival Papa would personally commend me for a job well done. Depending on his mood we could go between 120-160km.ph. and Papa enjoyed it.

I had to learn to adjust to a slower speed after the home-going of Papa when I began to drive Daddy Adeboye. He was not very comfortable with my speed. One day he sat me down and took me through per-minute/per-second calculations of the possibilities if a vehicle on top speed encountered any kind of sudden crisis. This knowledge made me to cut my speed whenever I was driving Daddy Adeboye. Our highest speed was between 100-110km.ph.

After the home call of Papa Akindayomi and I began to drive Daddy Adeboye, there was a time that something about his wife, Mrs. Folu Adeboye challenged me. This experience changed the whole course of my destiny. Shortly after the investiture of Adeboye as the General Overseer of RCCG, his wife decided to go back to school. And between 1983-84 she attended the RCCG Bible College. That was a big challenge to me: an elderly woman, a housewife and busy with other responsibilities finding time and putting herself together to go back to school.

I found it much food for thought. It occurred to me that if

I too made up my mind I could also develop myself beyond my present level. And naturally I love knowledge. One day I shared my heart yearnings with Daddy Adeboye who not only encouraged me but supported my ambition wholeheartedly. Therefore that year I enrolled at the RCCG Bible College. After my course I reported back to Daddy Adeboye to continue my driving job, but he made me to understand that now I had higher service to do for the Lord. Thus I moved from driver to pastor. Papa's life has been a big, unforgettable blessing to me.

"LOVING FATHER":
A NEPHEW'S REMINISCENCE
Ebenezer Olufemi Ademulegun

I came to live with Papa Akindayomi between 1966-68. My father Ademulegun was immediate elder brother to Papa. They were born of the same parents. Papa Akindayomi was somebody to whom his extended family meant so much, especially as regards our salvation.

GOD'S PROPHET

Rev. Akindayomi was a great prayer warrior. Therefore he was very prophetic. Thus if all Papa said to you was, *"my child it shall be well with you,"* just go to town and begin to celebrate with dance and drums because great things will suddenly begin to happen to you. Or if he looked at you and said, *"ah, landlord!"* it would not even matter if you did not have a plot anywhere nor money to buy. Because Papa had called you a landlord, you will surely become one. On the other hand if you made him angry and he said to you, *"but why have you done this to me?"* it's better you go to seek God's face because it would be terrible with you. Such was the power and authority of heaven with him. For example, he had kept talking about Pastor Adeboye's coming for at least five (5) years, before the man actually showed up physically. Yet he never knew him, nor his name nor anything about him, except his physical attributes as God had revealed them to him. He used to see incredible visions and he could hear the voice of the Holy Spirit so distinctly.

The very day Pastor E. A. Adeboye walked into our church at Ebute-Metta, Papa announced at workers' meeting, even before making Adeboye's acquaintance that his successor whom he had always talked about was here now, and we should stop praying for him to come! And today, we are all witnesses to the truth of that statement. Those days in church if Papa told anyone they would be baptised in the Holy Spirit that day, nothing could change that verdict, it would be so exactly. For instance, it was the same day he told me I would be baptised that I received the baptism. All Papa need do was lay his hand directly on your head and pray a very short prayer. It was automatic! All barriers would instantly give way. I believe the reason he doesn't struggle in his public ministry is because he spends so much time with God in secret.

PASSION

Conversion was Papa's greatest joy and desire. Even amongst his extended family he didn't hide this. Thus when you become converted, Papa's love for you knew no bounds and he would willingly do anything for you. In his ministry even when people came for healing, Papa's style was to make repentance from sin and conversion a pre-condition for praying for them. Despite all that God had revealed before Pastor Adeboye came, Papa still presented the salvation message to him first after their meeting.

Papa loved to talk about heaven, sing about heaven and preach about heaven. Therefore the central theme of any message he preached was holiness. He said only holiness would guarantee any believer heaven, and that it was the secret to answered prayer. Because Papa believed so much in prayer and its efficacy he brought up the whole church to know how to pray. If we as individuals or the church as a whole needed anything Papa's style was to lead us in specific prayers concerning such needs.

Afterwards he would tell us to begin to rejoice because since we prayed God had heard us. That meant the needs were already met. Interestingly after a few days miraculous supplies began to come for those things we had prayed. Papa never used to do appeals from the pulpit for church needs. Everything was settled in prayer. He would only announce the needs. Prayer was a very prominent part of the church life, because that was

Papa's life wire himself.

Moreover, for Papa deliverance wasn't a different or special ministry. His own style was that after the sermon the whole congregation hit the floor and began to pray with all their heart. In the course of such fervent prayers most problems, afflictions and difficulties were taken care of. And since there was no official stopping time for prayer, people were left to pray to their hearts' satisfaction. On most Sundays some people were still praying when we returned for the evening service at 6.00 p.m. The training in prayer made everyone to be up and doing in the prayer ministry. Thus the pressure of wanting to see Papa for every little problem was drastically reduced. As a matter of fact, outsiders put more pressure on him for prayers than his own people. The whole church was always like one strong army. No one was permitted to be weak.

Papa especially loved Sundays. His personal philosophy was that Sunday was the Lord's day in every sense of the word. In-between the evening service and after morning service we had different assignments to do for the Lord; visitation, evangelism, follow-up, etc. Papa told us we were not permitted by the Lord to spend His day for ourselves. Thus we hardly got home before 9.00 p.m on any Sunday.

AUTHORITY OF HEAVEN
It was always an experience to have Papa lay his hand upon your head for prayer. His touch was cool, soothing

and comforting. He did not sweat to pray. He would simply say, *"Go in peace, your affliction is over."* And often it was so. At a time my daughter was deathly sick. She stooled only watery discharge for 8 days non-stop. When I brought her to Papa for prayer, he laid his hands on her very gently and then gave her a shot of a special holy oil that he used to keep in his prayer room. When we got back home the child passed a greenish substance which was as hard as stone. When I picked up the thing and threw it against the wall with a great force, it bounced right back without breaking!

Having discharged that substance from her body, my daughter slept off! By the time she woke up she ate well for the first time in 8 days and began to amend. Afterwards she was never sick again.

"DRINK IT HOT!"
Papa Akindayomi was passionate about tea. He drank it everyday, and regardless of the time of day. Moreover you could only give tea to him in one way; bring the kettle directly from the boil. Papa could not drink tea with water from the flask. Never! For him that's cold. The kettle had to come straight from the fire with the water still bubbling. And when the tea had drawn Papa drank it straight. It was no more good if the first steam was allowed to escape. Papa taught me to drink tea because we used to spend so much time together. He was an incurable lover of tea.

When Papa served you tea he commanded you to start

drinking it instantly. You must not mind the steam because according to Papa hot tea was the cure for pile! Until you emptied your cup, Papa never allowed you to drop it. He would say, *"oya, drink it hot, drink it hot!"* This was the only way Papa himself drank his own tea; and I used to marvel at his incredible ability to drink such hot stuff.

A GREAT GIVER

I learned the virtue of giving from Papa. If he had anything that was up to two, you could be certain that he would soon give one away. He only needed to identify who was in need of it. Papa's life principle was that you must give in order to receive. He used to say that if he did not give away the one he has, new ones could not come in. One day I visited Papa and he showed me two shirts that had just been given him. He asked me to pick either one that I liked. I reluctantly did; because he was even willing to give me the two. When I visited him the following day he beckoned to me to show me the set of new shirts that had just been brought to him that day. Giving used to give him much joy.

MARRYING "BABA ALAKOSO'S" DAUGHTER: "YOU NEVER TAKE ANYTHING FOR GRANTED"
Pastor J. A. O. Akindele,
Former Asst. General Overseer (Admin/Personnel), RCCG

Both of us were in the choir, my wife and I. But at that particular time the discipline Papa instilled in his church members was such that when you woke up any morning you expected the coming of the Lord. Therefore our mentality was that the Lord could show up at any moment. As a result we never take anything for granted. That sense of urgency on us was such that we expected that the end could be even today. Everything we did therefore was with a lot of carefulness.

Male/female relations within the church were no less strictly monitored. Even though my wife and I were in the church choir, we see each other daily, we did everything together but that was as far as it went. We never talked nor tried to meet clandestinely anywhere. Because you see then if you as a brother were seen with a lady you would get a query from the church authorities. You would have to explain what your relationship with her was, especially if the two of you were alone without other church members being present. Therefore when you want to get married as a man you meet your leader. You must not talk directly to a lady in church on such matters. Under Papa's nose? You dared not!

As for Papa's daughter, Olubunmi whom I was interested in, it was a double hurdle. Papa knew exactly what time choir meeting ended. That means he had an idea when the girls in his house should get back home from choir practice. Besides Papa's house then was situated at No. 6, Kufeji Street, just behind the Casino at Rowe Park in Yaba. He had this curious practice of hiding in strategic corners around the Casino Cinema to observe his daughters on their way home from church. He could even show up at their back suddenly! You could never know when he would be there nor where he was hiding to watch, thus it was a very dicey affair to try to trifle with his girls; even if it was with good intentions. Knowing their father very well, the girls would not even entertain any talk with you. Fear of Papa's wrath was very palpable. He had a special way of caning his children that could never be forgotten in a hurry, including even his church pastors. He was a thorough disciplinarian.

When I was convinced that I had genuine interest in Papa's daughter, Olubunmi, I had to confide in a friend of hers, Sister Shade, wife of present A.G.O. (Family Affairs) Pastor Aderibigbe, who was Youth leader then. I did that with a lot of trepidation though, but I risked it because my wife was particularly close to Sister Shade. She it was who approached Aderibigbe on my behalf, and he encouraged us to begin to pray with Sister Shade so that we would know how to break through to Papa.

Subsequently Sister Shade invited Sister Olubunmi to her house one day and there I was waiting for her! My wife's only reaction was that I should tell Papa, but that was impossible! My wife confided in her mother, Mama Egbedire, who secured the assistance of Papa's close nephew Ebenezer Ademulegun, then in the police. Ademulegun broke the alabaster box for us and released the sweet smelling fragrance that we had been concealing.

It took a while but Papa eventually agreed to our

intended union and blessed it. As a result, here we are today. I thank God for Papa's exemplary life.

IN PAPA'S FOOTSTEPS:
LIVING WITH A HOLY MAN IN THE HOUSE
Pastor (Mrs) Durodoluwa Olukowajo
(Papa's first daughter)

Papa was a very important servant of God, committed, devout and completely sold out to God. It was an experience indeed to have lived under the same roof with such an unusual human being. I wouldn't have missed it for all the world!

For my father every other thing in this life lined up behind his call in God, and that included his family. Our home was an extension of the church in every sense of that word: the house was permanently full-the troubled, the sick, pregnant women, those facing the consequences of their total commitment to the Lord, the needy, etc. All roads led to Rev. Akindayomi's house and somehow there was space for all.

There was this Sister Eunice, an Ibo woman who lived with us for a very long time. The sister who was a young convert at Papa's new church became convicted of her position as a second wife somewhere and chose to restitute her ways. Subsequently she parked out. Afterwards this sister, not having where to turn to, landed in our house, and lived with us for very many years. She only left when the Lord eventually settled her and she got married to a pastor.

I learned the virtue of patience from Papa through his many trying experiences and how he handled them. One day I had complained to Papa that I didn't like my name: Durodoluwa *(i.e Wait on the Lord)*, anymore and thus would like to drop it. I was in primary school then and I told Papa that my schoolmates were laughing at me and calling me *"abiku"* (born-to-die child). Papa took time to explain to me how the Spirit of the Lord gave him that name even before I was born and why. It was during a Revival crusade and he had been singing to the crowd the song:

> *Duro d'Oluwa* (Wait upon the Lord)
> *Ma s'iye meji* (Do not be double minded)
> *Ohun k'ohun yo wu t'o le de* (Whatever be that comes)
> *Ore aye yi le ko wa sile* (Friends in this world may desert us)
> *Sugbon Jesu ko je gbagbe wa* (But Jesus never could forget us)

Ref: *Ah, ko je gbagbe wa!* 4(Ah, He could never forget us)
> *Ore otito o* (A faithful Friend is He)
> *Ah, ko je gbagbe wa* (Oh, He could never forget us)
> Aleluia!
> *Sugbon Jesu ko je gbagbe wa* (But Jesus could never forget us!)

You know Papa loves to sing. As he sang to the people

God told him, *'that's the name for the baby your wife is expecting.'* And that was it. So Papa pleaded with me that it was a covenant name and if I wanted God's covenant promises to work for me I should not reject it. Despite Papa's counsel I fought the name for years until I was getting married and they included it in my marriage certificate. However I observed that I always suffered anytime I didn't do my things with God's counsel. Therefore I learned to love and appreciate the virtue of patience by really waiting on the Lord before taking decisions. Today I really thank God for my name. It's been working for me!

In spite of Papa being a most loving father he was equally a very strict disciplinarian. His attitude was that no child would jeopardise his eternity and shame him before God. He also used to say that none would spoil his call by being wayward or ungodly. As a result he monitored our lives so closely and he was very, very strict with us. Most of his first examples started either with him or his children. For instance Papa started the practice of baby naming in church with me. The year was 1975 and I just had a baby. Normally baby dedication used to be in church but naming was in the baby's parents' home. Papa had increasingly become worried that his people were wont to throw caution to the wind and behave as the world during naming ceremonies, so he was seeking a good opportunity to check the trend.

On my baby's naming day, a Sunday, we were in the house preparing this and that for when people would arrive after church service, only for Papa's emissary to come from church and say that Papa was waiting for us and the baby right away. Why? Baby naming was now in church from that Sunday! I was initially angry but you know Papa was not somebody you disobeyed. The way he hears the Holy Spirit and responds made him a most unpredictable person, especially when it comes to the things of God. So though unprepared and finding it a little inconvenient we packed ourselves that day with the baby and reported in church. From that day Papa instituted the practice of baby naming in church early in the morning. Nobody was able to complain that Papa changed the former procedure because he started with his own family.

I BROKE INTO PAPA'S PREACHING!

On the Sunday that I had my baby an equally interesting episode occurred. I had given birth at the maternity *(just behind the church)* as early as 9:00 am but the placenta wouldn't come out. Everything that could be done at the maternity was done but nothing turned. For the next two hours I bled heavily and steadily while the leader of the church prayer warriors interceded non-stop until his jacket was sweat-soaked and had to be taken off him. It became clear that I was dying, and they soon removed me from the bed unto a mat on the floor. My blood gushed with such force that nothing could be used to pad me. The blood forcefully pushed off every stop and continued to pour.

My life gradually ebbed away. As I drifted in and out of

fainting spells I opened my eyes once again to see maternity attendants scooping my blood from all over the floor, yet Papa was just a close call away.

So I beckoned to one of the praying brothers to go tell Papa that his daughter was dying at the maternity. The man protested and said, "*But Papa is preaching right now. That's impossible!*" I replied and said, "*just go and tell him that Duro is about to die here o!*" When I insisted the man went. He had hardly stepped back in when Papa showed up behind him and without asking anybody what had been going on came straight at me on the mat. I just felt his cool hand on my stomach and I heard him cry out sharply, "*Father, release Your daughter in J-e-s-u-s name!*" It was a moment's touch and he got up. Almost immediately the stubborn placenta shot out of me and my bleeding stopped.

Papa did not even wait to see, because he left immediately back for the auditorium. No one in the congregation knew where he had been, many didn't even notice he left because when he got my message he had quickly rounded off his sermon and handed over the prayer part to one of his assistants.

A PROPHET INDEED
Papa used to say that God had showed him and told him at the start of his ministry how long he would do the work, how he would go and so on, but some of us didn't pay too much attention to such talk until Papa actually passed away. For instance six months before his demise

Papa called his tailor (now Pastor)Aderibigbe and told him he wanted a long white dress with long sleeves made. The man had no idea what Papa wanted to do with it. When he brought the dress Papa examined it and remarked: *"did you make this for the living or an angel?"* The man asked, *"Papa, don't you like it?"* As if joking with him Papa told Aderibigbe, *"anyway, don't worry, either an angel or a heavenly being can wear it sha."* With that Papa collected the dress and kept it away. It was shortly before his death that Papa showed Mama this same dress as his burial clothes!

Then in July 1977 Papa had just come back from a trip to Jerusalem and he mentioned that he was desirous of having a thanksgiving in church, especially as it was also his birth month (July). For someone that didn't believe in birthdays and ceremonies we felt that that was rather unusual; so my sister and I felt we should buy soft drinks in case people came to the house after the thanksgiving.

I took the request to Papa, but his reply to me was: *"Do you people want to have a birthday party? Don't worry, I guarantee you a big celebration. Then you can kill all the cows, buy all the drinks, arrange plenty of chairs and call plenty of people to celebrate with you, but not yet. That would be in 1980!"* Knowing his very proverbial ways I immediately informed my sister that I believe Papa had just hinted us that he would be passing away in 1980. She refused to believe it but I carefully filed away the information in my heart. Interestingly Papa died in 1980. This was a clear three years from when he had given the hint.

Ahead of his demise Papa also took his cousin, Ademulegun Snr., to his burial plot at Atan cemetery, letting the man know he was not to be taken to Ondo for burial. This he did because Ademulegun Snr. was the most senior of all his cousins and if he didn't hear it from Papa he alone had the family's authority to decide Papa's burial place without anyone contradicting him, including the church.

Then in April of 1980 a certain elderly woman in our church, called Mama Onasile, came to inform Papa that her daughter would be getting married at the Ebute Metta church on 6th December, 1980. Papa looked at her in a queer way and said to her, *"I advice that you change that date because headquarters will be too busy during that period and I doubt if a wedding will be possible.".* The old woman insisted that because of family considerations the date could not be changed. Papa tried further to change her mind, but when she would not be persuaded Papa relented and said, *"OK, let's wait and see."*

Eventually, having died in November of 1980, Papa's home going celebrations culminated in his burial on the 6th of December resulting in the (Onasile) wedding was shifted to the 13th of December, 1980.

I ENDED IN AGBEBI MINISTRY!
Papa started the *Agbebi* (maternity) ministry in RCCG, as a special calling from God. He never learned it from

anywhere and he told us that the Holy Spirit personally taught him, and always told him what to do. Delivery used to be taken in Papa's sitting room. Mrs Shade Aderibigbe (wife of present A.G.O Family Affairs) happens to be the first baby delivered personally by Papa in his sitting-room at the inception of the Agbebi ministry

Papa eventually trained Mama Egbedire who also trained many other women in the church, and these ones were later working with her. The way they went about it used to fascinate me so much that when I became a big girl I started assisting Mama in the work at home. Whether in the day time or at night Papa would know the exact hour that a woman would put to bed, and he would inform us. We would then make necessary preparations to take the delivery. Most times it was exactly as he told us. This became part of my fascination but as for being a career midwife, I consciously worked against the possibility. I never even wished to marry a pastor. Never!

The truth is Papa's early suffering as a pastor pitted me decidedly against ministry calling, more so the agbebi ministry that was so messy, stressful and demanding 100% attention on the pregnant women-spiritually and otherwise. Then initially all Papa had was a Raleigh bicycle and he would ride it all over town doing pastoral duties and visitation, sometimes while fasting and yet he would come back to supervise delivery. He never once came late! I didn't want all that trouble. Ignorantly I had felt it would always be like that- suffering all the way! But interestingly today one of my sons is a full-time pastor with RCCG and I'm excited about it. I gave birth to this boy three days after Papa's burial right on Papa's bed in his room.

As a man of God Papa fasted so frequently and he often made us to fast and also join the daily prayers at 9am, 12noon, 3 & 6pm. We hated the fasting so we would often sneak into the kitchen to drink garri, wipe our mouths then come out to join the prayers. Apart from that Papa used to call us together as his children to preach to us and also pray with us. It is in retrospect I see that those things were advance training for us: today I'm not only married to a pastor, but I'm a full time midwife in RCCG and loving the agbebi work. I hated the call when it came and struggled hard with it, but I remembered Papa's admonition about the covenant keeping God and therefore yielded. I have been using the agbebi work as an evangelistic tool to reach unsaved women who come to our maternity and I've been having great testimonies.

A GENUINE CALL & SUFFERING

I learned from Papa's life experiences that suffering is decidedly a part of the package of any genuine call. At a point all of Papa's initial twelve followers, but one, left and never came back, due to hardship. Secondly I saw from Papa's own responses to these things that it is attitude that matters the most. His mind was so made up that the obvious excruciating pain he was experiencing left, right and centre could not shake him.

Nothing seemed to be bad enough to discourage him.

Moreover I believe suffering actually comes because a genuine call must be proven. At moments of extreme challenges Papa used to say, "*Heaven is the goal. So let us continue in the race without slacking.*" For me that was a very valuable, and great lesson. It has helped me as an adult. Heaven is worth suffering for here on earth.

Papa told us when he came back from his first death experience that before he was turned back he was shown countless preachers who had missed heaven because of one avoidable lapse or the other. But he said the angels said to him: "*So that your own case would not be like those, you have to go back and make amends.*" It was after he had fully obeyed God's final instruction by going to apologise to Pastor Oshokoya that he got heaven's signal that the coast was clear now, and heaven was waiting for him.

That assurance was Papa's reason for rejoicing ahead of his home-going and also his reason for telling RCCG members to make the Sunday of his passing a day of thanksgiving in all our parishes. I believe Papa appreciated God's mercy to him in this regard, because he would have been too disappointed to have missed heaven, after all the suffering and sacrifices here on earth.

Papa's life showed me that when trouble comes one would either go back or do other things (i.e compromise) in order to survive, if they were not genuinely called in the first place, or if they would not pay the price for their calling. There's always a price and Papa paid his in full. Despite the trials and tribulation and trauma, he would always insist that God says he should never look back, whatever happens. And surely he did not. I salute his courage.

LIFE WITH MY FATHER
A DAUGHTER'S RECOLLECTION
Pastor (Mrs) O. O. Akindele *(Papa's 2nd daughter)*

Papa was a disciplinarian to the core and apart from that he had a certain awe about him because of his devotional lifestyle, so we used to be very afraid of him. Even Mama did not approach him anyhow. However when you come close you discover that Papa had a heart full of love. Our life at home with Papa was strictly regulated. Money was very scarce when he started because Papa never engaged in any secular employment, he was always a servant of God full time.

Good food was not in constant supply either while we made do with whatever clothes Mama could put together for us. Because she knew that Papa was completely sold out to God she was very supportive. Very often she would convert her head ties into long gowns for us girls when we were becoming bigger. At the early period of Papa's ministry he seemed to be detached from us in the sense that he did not get involved in domestic affairs. At this time, we the children were also not too close to him.

Papa had no personal belief in celebrating special occasions such as birthdays, Christmas, etc. He used to tell us at home that everyday we wake up should be a celebration before the Lord. We did not need to wait for any special days or dates. Thus in our house we did not even cook rice and chicken for Christmas! It was just like any other day. Whatever was available was what we ate with thanksgiving. Papa's favourite food *(being an Ondo man)* was pounded yam and bush meat. He used to eat once a day and that was in the evening. When he had finished eating, he would leave some of it for the person coming to clear the plates away.

Despite all the initial hardship at home Papa never for once flagged in his commitment and passion after the Lord. He believed that heaven would compensate for the sufferings of the now. And since we saw that that was his attitude to life, we also adopted the same at home and in other areas of our lives. Mama never complained. Rather she taught us to adapt to whatever our father liked.

MIRACLES GALORE
A very prominent part of the church ministry, the "*Agbebi*" (maternity) ministry came about in response to the needs of barren women within and outside the church. Papa was specially gifted in ministering to the barren, and we witnessed very many miraculous deliveries of babies.

If Papa prayed for the barren, they must become

pregnant. And once he told them after prayers, *"it's over, go home rejoicing"* that was always it. Even if their case was as protracted as twenty years, God would visit them. Part of Mama's duty was to follow-up with prayers and counselling such women from the point of conception until delivery time. Even though the doctrinal practice then was no drugs, God's faithfulness was evident as testimonies always followed the delivery cases. The Agbebi women took delivery of Pastor Adeboye's last son. Sometimes cases of long overdue pregnancies were brought to Papa for special prayers and God delivered them.

I remember a certain woman who was brought at a time said to have been pregnant for the past 2 years. Papa prayed for her and within 3 hours she gave birth to a healthy, normal baby. In Papa's prayer ministry, especially during the *Thursday Revival Hour* the lame walked, the blind saw, the deaf were set free. However miracles used to be downplayed for the salvation experience. Thus even when people got miracles, Papa emphasised to them that that was no guarantee of heaven. They must give their hearts to the Lord in repentance for their souls to be saved.

FEARLESS AND RESOLUTE

During the sand filling of the church at Ebute-Metta, the *omo oniles* (land owners/sellers) used to harass us a lot. Sometimes the Moslems around our church too would threaten us. On many occasions when Papa arrived the site he would find all kinds of *ebo* (fetish concoction, sacrifices) deposited at the church entrance or right in the centre of the new auditorium. Papa would kick everything out and tell the people to continue their work. He used to say that the forces of darkness would never prevail against God's Kingdom which we represented. The attacks never bothered him.

When he would not be deterred the attackers relented.

HEAVENLY-MINDED
Papa was a man detached from materiality. Mama and the rest of us had to pester him relentlessly before he reluctantly agreed to build one small house. He always told us that he didn't need a home here because his home was already waiting for him in heaven. At the time when Papa first died, he told us when he came back that God had showed him his home in heaven and that it was more beautiful than anything on this earth. He also said we should start praying to God to show us our own homes in heaven.

Papa did a curious thing one day, long, long before he died. He came back home that day in a somehow lighter mood and called for Mama. We were then living at Kufeji Street, in Yaba. Atan Cemetery was not very far from our house. Papa called his wife and said, "*I want to announce to you that I have bought some land somewhere today.*" Mama was cautiously excited, wondering who had worked on her husband and pulled off such feat. She replied him, "*oh is that so?*" "*Then we thank God o.*" Papa took her by the hand and said, "*come, I'll show you.*"

He went to a window towards the back of the house and pointed in a certain direction: it was the Atan Cemetery! Mama said, *"where is the land?"* And her husband explained himself better. He said to her: *"I have secured and paid for three burial plots-one is for me, one for you, and one for my friend."* Mama's reaction was not exactly joyous. She asked if Papa was planning to die now. Papa said, *"whether now or later, are we not going to die? I want to prepare for it, and I want to decide where I should be buried and how."* With that they both closed the subject for that day. But Papa was always more conscious of the day of death than his involvements on this material plane. One thing Papa also did was to have long showed to Mama the clothes he should be buried in, even before he was ever bedfast.

PAPA'S LOVE FOR ME

We all knew at home that Papa had a great hatred for sin and waywardness, but I used to be a quite restless youth. Papa had warned us on the pain of a curse never to think of marrying an unbeliever. He said we must only marry in the Lord and we must conduct ourselves properly. Despite this warning there was a time I stubbornly got involved with a certain unbeliever. When Papa got to know about it he sent me away from home. For a number of years I was banished from Papa's presence until I repented; and with the intervention of my uncle, Ademulegun (Senior) then in the Mobile Police, Papa took me back home.

Papa never spared the cane. He used to cane even his

pastors if they misbehaved. As a choir girl, one fellow came to visit me during choir practice one day and Papa got to hear about it. He caned me severely. After that day I told the man never to look for me again. What happened when I would marry Pastor Akindele was that I told Mama about his proposal because I was very afraid of Papa. Initially he told Mama no, but after some considerable time, he gave his consent. And that was how we were able to be married. Whatever you see of my life today has been the grace of God through Papa's efforts. I never thought I would amount to much in life because of my youthful restlessness, but Papa's love saw me through. I thank God for his life. He was a loving father.

"YOU WANT REDEEMED TO SACK US?"
THE CRY OF A FAITHFUL DISCIPLE
Pastor Mrs. Folu Adeboye, (*General Overseer's wife*)

The new generation Redeemites would find this hard to believe, but the present liberty and freedom of worship they enjoy today took the battle of a lifetime to achieve. In the vanguard of the conflict was no less a personality than Pastor (Mrs.) Folu Adeboye herself (*a.k.a Mummy G. O*)!

Rev. Akindayomi's classical mode of worship needed to be amended as the church's profile expanded beyond the old and conservative folk, but some would rather insist on the old school. At that year's (Holy Ghost) Congress in Ado-Ekiti, Pastor John Omewa (*a fine musician,* formerly with the late Afro-Beat Maestro, Fela Anikulapo Kuti), came to the Congress with powerful Conga drums. They were to be used during praise/worship session! Nobody believed it. *Drums? In Redeemed?* In panic Mummy G. O screamed at Pastor John, *"John, you want Redeemed to sack us?"* Only recently she was a witness to the conflict that resulted from (Pastor) Adeboye's permitting the clapping of hands after teaching the people from Psalm 47, pointing out that it was OK for God's people to clap to Him. An elderly deaconess was ready to take Pastor Adeboye up for daring to touch the Papa Akindayomi doctrine of no clapping, dancing and drumming. Another elder had to get up and declare his readiness to dance even to *Gbedu* (Yoruba cultic drum), should it be brought to church, before the matter was finally resolved. The dust had hardly settled, and now this: *"I'm going to tear those drums myself!"* , Mummy G.O. declared to Pastor John. *"No Mummy, you will not tear the drums. We will only use them here, but we won't bring them into the church in Lagos,"* replied Pastor John.

And so the drums were used at Ado-Ekiti, and subsequently at other meetings but with much caution and carefulness. Today the story is different. *"Thanks,"* in the words of Pastor (Mrs.) Adeboye, *"to God Who has intervened in the worship of the Redeemed Christian Church of God."*

CHAPTER SEVEN

PAPA...

REMEMBRANCES OF HIS LIFE

"OMO BABA JESU N PE O"
John Kolade Akindayomi *(Papa's first surviving son)*

IT WAS AN EXPERIENCE INDEED BEING A part of Papa's life and household. He was an embodiment of godliness, discipline and love. Interestingly however as kindhearted as he was Papa never joked with his cane. I say that because I was often at the receiving end of that cane as a result of my youthful rascality.

One day I made the greatest mistake of my life by coming home drunk. I was grown up at this time and had started working. When I arrived home Papa was sitting by the door and I never even thought he noticed my tipsy state. As I made to pass by him he called me and said, *"Please come in and bring my purse over there."* I turned in but the next I felt was a sharp whip lash across my back! The impact was like live wires. Papa was unhappy with me, and unfortunately for me it fell on one of his several fasting periods. So for the next three days Papa locked me in with himself and made me fast without food or water. I nearly died of hunger, but Papa told me, *"If you could enjoy alcohol for all night why, you can also enjoy this one too for a few days."* Until the third day he never let me out of his sight because we were in that room together night and day.

Papa wanted everyone to go to heaven and this became his main focus in life. To my mind this all-consuming passion somehow slanted Papa's views in other areas. For instance Papa would rather spend all monies coming into his hands on Gospel matters and church people than on us. This particularly affected our education negatively because as money comes Papa was already thinking of what crusade or outreach to use it for. If we complained he would reply by saying that, *"don't you know these souls would perish if we didn't reach out to them?"* He was of the opinion that heaven would compensate for all losses. Yes, but I think education is very important on this side of eternity before we get to heaven.

I believe though that Papa's disposition to this all important issue was a function of the level of his own understanding at that time, because Papa was a most loving, and caring father. Later in life he tried to compensate us by doing everything within his power to make us happy and fulfilled at whatever vocation we found ourselves eventually and he always gave us as much money as we asked for, even despite that we were adults now and working.

As a man of God Papa was a great pastor and a rugged evangelist. He travelled often on evangelistic campaigns to different parts of the country. These journeys he called *"tours"* and on the few occasions I went with him I witnessed unbelievable miracles and wonderful manifestations of the Divine presence with Papa. The experience is unforgettable.

Because of Papa's love for souls he had a sticker made with the wording: **Jesu N Pe O** (i.e. *Jesus is Calling You*), this he pastes on his cars so that when you see Papa's car, the first thing that confronts you is that Jesus is calling you. Besides, as Papa is discussing with someone-no matter the subject- he's looking for a way to bring it round to the matter of the person's soul. He believed everyone could be saved and that it was his duty to tell them about that possibility. Because of that sticker and Papa's constant preaching to people in the neighbourhood, in most places we lived people would call us *"awon omo baba Jesu n pe o"*, i.e. "The children of baba Jesus is calling you."

Nothing in this world, including his children could stand between Papa and church matters. He was so attached to God. Any child that would not co-operate with him was made to do so any way Papa could make them. It was his habit to pray for us wholeheartedly and I believe God heard those prayers. Papa did not want us to end up in hell, thus if he was sitting down or walking along the road or whatever else his mouth constantly moved in prayer. And the old man could fast! It was possible to count the total number of days Papa ate in a whole year. There was a day I went to him and said, *"Papa but why won't you eat now? You look so emaciated because of constant fasts!"* He just smiled at me indulgently and asked if I didn't know that fasting was the source of power.

STRICT PARENT

Papa was a stickler for rules and presenting matters plainly before all. So in our growing years it was difficult to escape with questionable moves under Papa's ever sniffing nose. He even used to search our rooms sometimes in case we had come home with things that didn't belong to us. I remember once that I had borrowed a friend's shirt for an outing and came home with it. As I arrived Papa noticed that I was wearing a strange apparel and he accosted me. When I told him where I got it he asked me to return it right away and never let him see a repeat of the action. He said, *"How will I know when you will even bring things that have been stolen home? Soon you will not be satisfied with anything you have but other people's things."* I returned the shirt that night because I wasn't allowed into the house.

At another time when I had started working, my supervisor at work, a white man allowed me to take away some office furniture that had been discarded. When I arrived home with the whole lot, Papa asked me the origin of the load, and I told him. The following day

Papa followed me to work with the stuff, and asked to see my supervisor. After the man had explained to Papa that he gave me leave to take them away, Papa asked him if he was the owner of the office furniture, and on that note told the man that I could not be allowed to keep them.

One day I went out to a party from work and came a little behind the 10' o clock deadline that Papa had given me before I left home. I was actually close to the gate by 10p.m but because I wasn't yet inside the compound Papa did not permit me to come in and I slept outside that day. All of Mama's pleas that I be allowed in did not move Papa, he said I flouted his instruction. Knowing that Mama could be more compassionate as a woman, Papa went to his room with the gate key and only released it in the morning. I tell you Papa was tough!

I went to join the Nigerian Army in anger and frustration because I wanted to leave home but what I discovered was that Papa's prayers followed me everywhere. You know that was during the Nigerian civil war and I had expected to die at the war front or something, but strangely that was not to be. Rather than die I kept being promoted and I became an instructor in my unit instead. I believe this was a function of Papa's prayers for me.

TRAVELLING EVANGELIST
On most journeys Papa went in pursuit of Kingdom business he often had interesting encounters, and it was a great priviledge to have been with him on some of the

trips.

Sometime around 1969 or so we were coming to Lagos from Benin and all of a sudden our car stopped because the fuel had finished. When the driver told Papa what the problem was Papa told us to come down and as we did we saw a flowing stream nearby. Papa said to his driver (not Mulero): *"Go and take from that flowing fuel and put in the tank and let's get out of here."* The driver had worked so long with Papa and become used to his ways so he simply did as he was told. I watched him take of the flowing water, put in the tank and start the engine. The thing roared back to life and we were soon on our way. It's incredible but we drove with water in the car as petrol until we arrived Lagos where we drove into a filling station, drained the remaining water and put petrol. Papa did not even act as if anything out of the ordinary had happened. To him it was normal to live in the supernatural.

This next one he told us himself. Papa said while on tour the car was on high speed when it suddenly skidded off the road and ended in a deep and narrow gully far into the bush. Miraculously he came out unscathed but with the car buried in the ditch. He said how he came out was a mystery even to him. Did angels bring him out? He didn't tell! However because of his miraculous escape Papa said the car should not be removed. Therefore till today the car stays in that ditch.

NATURALLY SUPERNATURAL

Witnessing miracles with Papa was almost a common thing. Not that he took it for granted but I mean that the miraculous was his normal lifestyle. One day Papa had taken the whole family home to Ondo and we were on our way back to Lagos. You know he loves speed but not with the whole house in the car. So it was not as if the driver was over-speeding on this particular day, but shortly after leaving Ibadan our left rear tyre went burst! We heard a loud noise as the thing gave way. The car tried to skid but Papa told the driver not to stop but just go on steadily. The driver said, *"But Papa we have a burst tyre."* Papa said, *"No it is not my tyre that burst, just keep moving."* The driver went ahead obediently even though the car started to go zigzag on the road, and was giving some distress sounds.

We were worried that probably the bare rim was grinding on the asphalt, but since Papa had said no stopping the driver continued on the journey. Interestingly the car seemed to suddenly balance again on the road and we drove on smoothly as if nothing was wrong, and we weren't hearing the disturbing noise again. We drove safely all the way to our house in Mushin without any incident. As we got out of the car we all watched as the damaged tyre made a hiss and went flat. The driver simply went over and changed it.

Once I was with Papa on tour going from Oshogbo to Ibadan. We had gone quite far into the journey and the driver was cruising. All of a sudden the axle gave way and our car entered the bush. Of course it got stuck there. What to do? Papa instructed us to get out of the car. He then told the driver to go and get a beam from a nearby tree. When he came with it Papa said: *"Now tie that to the axle and let's go."* The man followed Papa's instruction and that was how we got out of that jam. We drove with the piece of wood like that all the way to Ibadan and we had no problems. Nothing seemed to be strong enough to deter Papa from his set course at any time and in any way. He always found a way.

I can also remember a day that we were going with Papa on tour and the car wiring caught fire. We could see smoke already coming out of the bonnet. The driver wanted to get out of the road and park when Papa said, *"No, don't stop. The One that sent me on errand is the owner of this car it can't catch fire. Go on!"* True to Papa's command the driver went on and at a point we just saw that the smoke had fizzled out and we didn't even know how the fire died. I'm not sure again whether it was during this particular tour that Papa raised one dead man. The man's relations were passing by with the corpse and Papa accosted them and asked them to put him down. He prayed and the man came back to life. This incident was sometime in 1969 or 1970.

There was a day Papa was holding a crusade and the clouds gathered as if the rains would fall presently. In a short while it started to drizzle. Papa raised his hand toward heaven and said, *"Rain I'm busy now. This meeting must hold."* Afterwards he resumed what he was doing and in a few minutes the drizzle stopped completely and there was not a drop until the end of that meeting. Rather the sun began to shine. At another time we were having (Holy Ghost) Congress at Ondo and the rain began to fall. Papa did not pray, but only said: *"Rain, not today."* And that was it. The rain ceased almost instantly.

One day a certain middle-aged woman ran to Papa in panic. Her house somewhere on Bola Street at Ebute Metta was vibrating so violently it seemed ready to collapse. She was on the verge of packing out of the place. The trouble was that some persons were contending for the property with her and she felt probably they were using diabolical powers to torment her away. As she told her story Papa asked her: *"Do you believe that Jesus is alive?"* The woman answered an emphatic *"Yes"*, and Papa told her, *"Now let's go to your house."* On arrival Papa placed his foot on the entrance of the property and prayed a very short prayer. As a matter of fact the house had tilted to a very grotesque angle. But Papa told the woman after praying, *"Take possession of your house. No evil will befall you."* She hardly believed it but took Papa's word by faith even though it took some time for her to take full possession of the house again. In the meanwhile all the terrifying signs had disappeared. The woman though quite old now is alive till today and still living in that same house.

The occurrence of miracles in church or at the house when Papa prayed for people was hardly news anymore.

When the church was still at Willoughby Street, Papa had varied ways of ministering to the people as led by the Holy Spirit. He had this rod he used to hold sometimes, and any day he held it and said God told him not pray, extra special miracles used to occur. Papa would tell the people that God said they should just touch his clothes and they would receive their miracles. On one such occasion Papa was wearing a very beautiful, big *agbada*, and the people kept coming and touching, but rather than touch some were pulling at his dress. By the end of the service Papa's agbada had got torn in several places, but I personally witnessed a leper who touched his clothes that day and was healed instantly.

AUTHORITY AND THE SECRET OF IT

Papa was a man who had so much authority with God and it was clear to all. Whenever we wonder to him aloud how he seemed to have a literal open cheque with God, Papa often said the secret was a life of holiness. He would say, *"You have to live above sin and hate sin if you must have power with God."* He said if we abhorred sin and the appearance of evil whatever we say would be exactly so.

I remember a man that Papa made some pronouncements upon, who when things began to happen could hardly contain himself. The man in question was so unusually short that even children gathered to stare at him whenever he was passing. He was more or less a midget. Papa met this man at Ilorin (Kwara State) during a crusade.

The man came to Papa on one of the nights and confided in him that his perennial embarrassment was lack of a wife which had become a mirage because of his shortness and size. No woman wanted him; therefore he wanted Papa to pray for him. Rather than pray Papa looked at him and said, *"Why won't you marry? I assure you that by this time next year you'll be with your own wife. The Lord will show you the person and you will recognise her. Afterwards you will build your own house and you will never have to live in a rented apartment again."* The man stared at Papa in amazement, but believed and he vowed that if it should so happen he would give a piece of land to God's work. At the time Papa spoke to the man he was a senior civil servant.

True to Papa's prophetic declaration this man got promoted to the post of a Permanent Secretary in the ministry, and then in a short few months he met his wife, a teacher, who was above five feet tall. On his wedding day he had to be carried unto the seat beside his wife. That was how short he was. He had for wedding shoes the Dunlop type of bathroom slippers because his feet were too tiny for any shoe size. But the Lord honoured the word of His servant to the short man.

The man was so elated at the turn of events that he made good his vow unto the Lord. It was on the land he gave that the first RCCG Parish, which became the headquarters was built in Ilorin. His own personal house was built directly behind the church and he became a very faithful member of RCCG.

Among the five children born to him by his wife was a set of twins-a boy and a girl. All but two of the children were of standard height.

Another interesting story I remember is that of Rev. Thompson, who is about 80 or so now. This man's Mum was Papa's neighbour when he was young and he said his mother used to bring him to Papa regularly for prayers. So he said he was preparing for a particular exam one time and his mother brought him to Papa as usual. Papa did not pray, he only said to the young man: "*Go you have already passed! You have made all the papers.*" He said when he went for the one hour exam he finished it long before the stipulated time, because as he took the exam paper he saw as it were in a vision all the answers to the questions. These he copied down and afterwards went to submit his answer sheet. He said the invigilators became suspicious thinking that he had seen the questions ahead and smuggled in the answers. They subsequently searched him but found nothing incrimination on him.

Even after becoming an adult this man was so close to our family and could never have enough of Papa's company. Until we moved from that area of Lagos even after Papa's passing away he was still close to us, always talking about Papa and his power with God.

That igunnu (*masquerade*) story Pastor Mulero told you, what he didn't remember to tell you was that before they ran away Papa had told them that if they stayed too long (*arguing with Mulero*) fire would descend upon them, and

174

as they were still contemplating what to do a fire actually broke out in the air right over their heads. One of them that even tried to throw charms in Papa's direction had his right hand suspended in mid-air. This became too much for them and thus they ran for dear life! I was around at home that day and witnessed the incident.

Papa's power and authority with God was such that it was a risky venture to stand against him as a leader. I remember that during the testy transition period when some persons were not happy that he might be handing over to a relatively new comer and a much younger man, God's reaction quickly checked the trouble shooters. There was one of the men in strong opposition to Papa's moves whose wife died suddenly and shortly after he lost one of his children. Papa made it a point of duty to start fasting and praying unto God for this elder asking for God's mercy on his behalf.

PAPA'S PASSING AWAY
Papa did some interesting things shortly before his death which make me to still respect his relationship with God till today.

Normally any time my wife got pregnant Papa would send us a name for the expected baby. But for the baby born a few days to Papa's passing away, much as I troubled him, Papa said he had no name for the baby yet. However a few days after the baby was born Papa agreed to give a name asking us to bring the baby boy to him in Lagos for his blessing. After praying for the baby he said his names would be Stephen Oluwatunmibi. Usually Mama would ask him the meaning of the names or why he gave them. On this occasion he told Mama that Stephen was in honour of Steve Rathod, the white man he ordained. When we asked him for the meaning of the other one, Papa said, *"All of you go and p ray and let God tell you the meaning."* He never told us why he gave that name which literally translates to: *"God has given birth to me again."* Papa died a few days after naming this baby, whose birth was on October 21, while Papa's passing occurred on November 2, 1980, twelve days apart. I believe Papa knew he was leaving soon and felt comforted that a new baby boy was born about the same time into his family.

On the eve of his passing Papa literally shooed me away to my base at Ibadan. I'd been around for the whole week just to see him, but by Saturday Papa suddenly said I should start making plans to go back. But I said no I would rather stay. This was after we had had a meal of his favourite pounded yam together with Mama. When I protested Papa said, *"Have you forgotten that tomorrow is thanksgiving in all Redeemed churches? I want you to do your own thanksgiving in Ibadan. Besides remember the tour I had told you about. I should take the journey soon. When I come back I will see you."* I never realised that Papa was actually telling me a final bye-bye. I reluctantly went back to Ibadan only to be recalled after the thanksgiving on Sunday with news that Papa had transited by the break of day. The truth is that's a man I could never forget! I miss him greatly.

DAD IN MY HEART
Pastor Ifeoluwa Akindayomi

It is interesting that though I was Papa's last child, but I did not live completely with him. As a matter of fact I left home at age twelve and only came back at 17, on the occasion of Papa's passing away.

Now what happened? I was caught one day in a rude behaviour to my senior sister, Titi (now Mrs. Adewale) to the hearing of some elderly people in church at Ebute-Metta. Thus Rev. Fajemirokun and wife specially requested Papa to release me to them so as to prevent my becoming a spoilt brat. Papa readily and willingly gave his total consent to the idea. Thus I started living with this couple at Palm-Grove Estate, from 1975. I only returned to our place in 1980 when Papa died.

WHAT I REMEMBER OF HIM
STRICT AND METICULOUS
Papa was a very strict person. He was strict with himself, with people around him and with the running of the church. For example in our house, Christmas was not necessarily a special event requiring that we buy anything special, not shoes, dress or even rice and all. You dare not walk up to Papa and demand special things for Christmas because your friends or other children around are buying things. Rather Papa gave out many things in the house to the needy at this festive period.

Then in our household Sunday was the Day of the Lord:

a very special day and wholly devoted unto the Lord. Therefore as a member of Papa's household you don't buy anything, nothing at all on Sundays.

Whatever you know you would need for Sunday must have been purchased by Saturday evening. If Papa should hear it that a member of his household did any kind of transaction(s) on a Sunday the person would be in serious trouble.

CHURCH MATTERS

Papa was extremely meticulous and vigilant with everything that has to do with the church. The church was not very big then but you couldn't bring any kind of money to church and have Papa accept it. He used to say he didn't want bad money. He was always interested in the quality of the people's Christian life and testimony. For instance if someone suddenly began to bring large amounts of tithe to the church Papa would send for the person. They must account for where they got such funds. If their explanation was not satisfactory or it was questionable the money was returned to the giver.

Papa's emphasis was never money, for (church) projects, it was always the people. During the construction of the church facilities anyone that didn't have money was advised to come and donate time doing manual labour in lieu of money. Emphasis was on getting the job done not on collecting money. This particular aspect of Papa's style used to anger some of the people working with him then, but he wasn't bothered. He was so consistent with this pattern that even when the church had started to have Parishes and the finances of the church improved somewhat Papa did not change. Therefore he had a few unhappy ones among his associates, who felt that his eagle-eye supervision of the church's finances was too stringent. It didn't allow for anyone playing any form of games with church funds.

When Pastor (E. A.) Adeboye came in, and some of Papa's closest aides saw the way Papa was going on with him, their own personal expectations of succeeding Papa started to crumble fast. And this boiled over unto the first major open confrontation with Papa over who takes what.

Papa's closest assistant who happened to be his very close friend, and they're also from the same state, quarreled publicly with Papa because Papa insisted that he must give financial account of the parishes he was overseeing. Secondly it was now apparent to this man that he would not be named as Papa's official next-in-command. Thus at that year's Ministers' Conference he flared up, and angrily walked out. Subsequently this elderly man left the Redeemed Church altogether and never came back.

Apart from that case, some other pastors sometimes would threaten to leave with their parish. And Papa would tell them, *"The church belongs to God."* *"You want to take the parish and carry the people?"* *"Please go, and take anything you want with you, because God has not called me to fight with anybody."* He never once personally got involved in any case of power tussle; no matter how big or strategic the parish being wrested from him was. It is interesting to note that some such men who left in this manner sometimes sneak into the Redemption Camp ground today to attend Holy Ghost Congress. But they're not in situations and conditions that they would love to be seen or identified publicly anymore.

PAPA'S LIFESTYLE
NOTHING HE CAN'T GIVE OUT
Mama used to get angry with him sometimes but Papa could never be deterred when it comes to giving. There was nothing he couldn't give out, even his cars. As soon as they're given to him he's already thinking of who to give them to. Nothing was sacred. For instance it was his tradition at every Annual Convention to give out all his suits, and shoes. Everything! Normally he would hang them out in a place and call on his pastors to go in and take whatever they wanted for themselves. He derived so much joy from doing this. I still pray to have his kind of a large heart.

His non-attachment to material things was such that he had to be forced to build the only house he had. Technically he didn't even own it because the plot of land was paid for by Rev. Fajemirokun who also started to build it. He persuaded Papa that it was not a wrong thing to cease being a tenant, now that the church was doing quite well. It took the man's combined efforts with Mama for Papa to show any interest in the house idea.

And at that it only got to decking level and then he left it. This was where Papa lived until his death.

After Papa's death, Pastor E. A. Adeboye felt that Papa should have a house back at Ondo, and so a modest place was built in his name there also. Aside from these Papa had no personal landed property anywhere. He was completely uninterested. As for the mighty oak called RCCG, Papa had made all his natural children to understand that it is not a family church, we don't own it. The church belongs to the Lord. Therefore as Papa's children we're pleased to serve within the church structure as members, not owners. Papa never gave us such an idea.

The plot of land where my house is built at the Redemption Camp was the one allotted to Mama. She gave me permission to build it in her lifetime. RCCG is not our family property. Our family's ultimate desire is to see RCCG become what God told Papa it would become. Therefore we're happy to abide by his ideals, goals, and beliefs.

CONFRONTATIONAL
Papa was not your good example of what we would today call diplomatic or tactful at all. He wasn't by any means politic. People saw him as being too confrontational, and honestly that was what he was, and more. He didn't know how to respect persons. He used to say that before God everyone was equal. As a result if you were not sure of your facts do not go to report anybody to him over any

matter. As soon as you have made your report he would sit you down and call another person to go call the other person. Then he would say to you in the person's presence, *"yes, this is brother or sister so & so, please could you tell me again what you said he/she did or said?"* God help you if you could not repeat or sustain your allegations. Thus idle tales, rumour and time-wasting stories didn't ever find their ways into Papa's presence, because people knew he would investigate openly.

Don't come late to Papa's church, and march straight to the front. He hates it! If you come late, sneak in quietly and never let the old man see you. Otherwise, no matter who you are, you will get it from him that day. Papa could talk to anybody as occasion demands. At home if you were not ready when Papa was, you will not go in the car with him, yet you must not arrive church late. Papa never goes late for anything anywhere.

As loving a pastor as Papa was, misbehaviour was not treated discreetly by him. A member's sin was judged openly and the person was disciplined before all. Even if the case was as terrible as stealing or sexual sin, Papa spelled it out and made the offender to sit outside the church auditorium for a number of Sundays. He said that was better than sending them away, from hearing the Word of God and fellowship.

UNCEREMONIOUS
It surprised many to hear that Papa had bought his own burial plot, and made arrangements how he was to be

Papa J. O. Akindayomi

Mama Akindayomi rejoicing
before the Lord at the Holy Ghost service

Papa's three daughters: Titilayo (now Pst. Mrs. Adewale),
Olubunmi (now Pst. Mrs. Akindele), and Durodoluwa (now Pst. Mrs. Olukowajo)

White men and women worshiping the Lord
at one RCCG's conventions - a prophecy fulfilled

Papa laying in state at the church

Simple, polished wood coffin (*in accordance with Papa's last wishes*)

Mama Egbedire having a last look at her companion
of so many intriguing years

Rev. Josiah Olufemi Akindayomi lying-in-state,
surrounded by family members

E. A. Adeboye, acting as interpreter for the last
time-during Papa's funeral service

Ministers at Papa's funeral service: E. A. Adeboye *(left)*
staring into a heavily pregnant future

Church members watch in rapt attention as Papa's
remains are being taken away for burial

Papa's funeral procession, led by the church choir

Motorcade on the Ebute Metta highway towards Atan Cemetary

Rev. Josiah Olufemi Akindayomi (1909-1980)

buried long before he died. The plot he purchased at the Atan cemetery was the special multiple-tier type that could take more than one person at a time. Even though it is permanent and could never be re-used for another person, but Papa's reasons for doing things that way were different.

Papa said the plot was for himself, Mama and one of his close aides, who was also his personal friend, Rev. Talabi. This Rev. Talabi died first, and then Papa in 1980, and Mama in 2001, and that is the order in which they were buried. Papa was buried with his head covered with the head piece of his Jerusalem Pilgrim's outfit in accordance with his last wishes. He said he was to be buried in a simple, polished wood coffin with no special effects at all. Why all the fuss? Remember that Papa used to be a C&S Prophet. And back there he had strongly disagreed with the idea of turning the founder's burial site into a kind of a shrine. No matter what they would say, Papa said he saw the practice from the perspective of God's Word as idolatry.

This was Papa's background, and undoubtedly this was one of the principal errors that God wanted him to depart from by calling him out of the C&S. In order to forestall a probable repeat of the errors of the old order therefore, Papa made sure that nothing out of the ordinary was allowed to be done about his burial site. It was deliberate. He didn't want his burial place to be turned into what it is not.

God hates idolatry so much that He has pronounced very terrible judgment upon it (see Lev.18: 5; Rev. 21:8). Turning any place into a sacred place by personal design is always a sin before God because such places become the equivalent of what the Word of God calls *"high places."*

These high places become altars raised unto strange gods *(demonic spirits)* other than the living God. A king of Israel, Jeroboam the son of Nebat became especially detestable before God because of this practice, and God could never forget his sin (see I Kg. 12:27-33). Jeroboam chose a place, decided a day and month and ordained the strange feast. But the Word of God says, **"And this thing became a sin"** (I Kg. 12:30). Jeroboam did not end well nor did he have an enviable legacy before the Almighty God (see I Kg. 14: 7-16). God hates idolatry with a special hatred.

DEATH AND OUR FAMILY
THE DEATH OF BROTHER DEJI
I was old enough to remember the death of my elder brother, Deji in 1978. Papa and brother Deji were very close and Papa loved him very much because he was a very dutiful son. He was also a kind person. I remember he bought our first fridge at home then, because he was already working with Leventis Motors. His passing away affected Papa rather badly. As a matter of fact, I believe Papa started falling sick off and on ever since that incident. He really took it to heart.

Out of about thirteen or so children that Papa had in his lifetime only five of us are alive today.

DEATH ARRESTED

It was not a very happy realisation in our family that death kept depleting us even while Papa was still alive. No less concerned was Papa himself. Therefore before he finally passed away Papa specially addressed the issue and spoke into our lives, by declaring to his remaining children that none of us would ever die young again. He arrested the scourge of death and took it away with him. Being the last born of the family I made sure I celebrated it therefore when I turned 40. I told people I broke tradition (*of no elaborate celebrations*) just to attest to God's faithfulness to Papa's last words that we would no more be dying young. Papa's prayer always work, and this one was a particularly special one to him.

PAPA'S DEATH

Even though I was no longer living at home with Papa some five years before he died but I always saw him whenever I wanted to. He was very fond of me. I attended a boarding school, and came to the Fajemirokun's during holidays but I found my way to Papa any time I wanted.

On this particular day I was in the dining hall at school and I just felt like seeing Papa. It was a Thursday. I left directly from the dining hall for home. Unknown to me Papa had been ill. On arrival I met the Church's prayer squad who had been on a long prayer chain since Papa took ill. They prayed round the clock for Papa, in different shifts at our house. I asked to see Papa and they showed me directly into his room.

Papa was lying full length on his bed. When he saw me he said, *"ah welcome, I've been expecting to see you."* I was happy to see him too. After a while he brought out his wallet and handed it to me and said, *"Take everything in it. I give it to you."* Mama was there, so she took the wallet from me and rather gave me some of the money instead. However I continued staying with Papa. It was now well past midnight and he told me to go in and sleep but I told him I still wanted to stay with him, so he let me be. Early the next morning I left for school. And that was the last I saw of Papa alive. By the break of Sunday morning, *(two days later)* Papa had gone home to glory. On Monday morning, Papa's driver (Pastor) Mulero came to pick me in school, telling me Papa wanted to see me. But I told him, *"Papa has never sent before that he wanted to see me. Surely Papa is dead."* Although Pastor Mulero tried to make me think otherwise but I told him I knew Papa was dead. When we arrived the house I saw that it was so. Pastor (E. A.) Adeboye took me into his own room in our house and comforted me.

DO I MISS HIM?
I particularly miss Papa's prayers more than any other thing, because even though everyone else at home would want to spoil me, but never Papa, so I don't miss that about him! But Papa was a mighty man of prayer. People would throng him for prayers and they were

never disappointed.

As a young boy just living my own life and seeing Papa's prayer life I always had this confidence that my father was there praying for me. If you knew nothing else about Papa you knew he was a man of prayer. Papa taught us to pray to God on our knees. His prayers were mighty. And oh how I miss that! In those days because Papa would be ministering tomorrow he would not sleep throughout the night. You could hear him praying in the night. And he was fervent, he didn't pray gentleman's prayers at all. He would study his Bible and pray; and leave directly from his prayer room to church. Papa believed that ministering to people was a work of the Holy Spirit and there was no way to do it effectively outside the Holy Spirit's involvement. He used to say it was the Holy Spirit that would talk.

My father's devotional life resulted in such a high standard of holiness that I still covet. Today I see much of Papa's prayer style and life of holiness in his successor, Pastor E. A. Adeboye. Sometimes I see him on his way to his nightly prayers at the camp and I would only see him coming back the following morning, yet he beats some of us also living at the Camp to morning prayer meetings in town! Whenever I think about these things I always reflect that the present Overseer has completely imbibed Papa's spirit. The transfer of mantle was excellently done.

CHALLENGE OF MY FATHER'S LEGACY

You know I was not always a good boy because I was Rev. Akindayomi's son. I lived my own life and did things I felt meant the good life. Daddy Adeboye's first son, Deolu is my bosom friend and we sowed our wild oats together doing all kinds of rascally things. However we always had a problem: our fathers were godly men and we were ever conscious of that. It hung around us like a shadow. Therefore whenever we went clubbing we would never sit in the open. We played "safe" by hiding in the VIP sections of the club. Redeemed wasn't as big as this then, but we still would not like to be seen by anyone because we were pastors' children.

We knew our lifestyles were wrong. Whenever we got back home from any outing we would avoid being seen, because the tell tale effects of alcohol could give us away, so we would take care to brush our teeth vigorously and hide our breath under heavy doses of mint sweets. But as the years went by we both realised that we could never continue in a lifestyle of sin and ungodliness. Thus we eventually repented and became born again at about the same time.

After I became born again I became more conscious of my responsibility as the son of a very godly man. Besides I discover that people easily link my behaviour and actions to my father's name. That became a huge check on my every action-wherever I am and with whom. I have to live a gentleman's life, and that option, for me is a blessing.

PROUD TO BE A PASTOR

When I was still a very young boy I loved to imitate Papa by preaching in the house. I would find any object that could represent a microphone and start to preach to an imaginary congregation. In Papa's style I would have someone stand by me as my interpreter. Papa and Mama used to be so excited about that and Mama would even insist that I could not be anything else but a pastor. When I eventually started secondary school I told Papa I would like to become a pastor and he was very happy about my desire.

Even though I had challenges along the way, but despite all odds, today I am a pastor. I am so glad that I have fulfilled my word to my parents, and have achieved Mama's dream for me. God has helped me especially in this regard.

PAPA'S LIFE STILL A BLESSING

During the Convention a few years ago an elderly man walked up to me at the Redemption Camp and asked to have a word with me. He told me that Papa had given him a suit as a young man and he wore the thing until it was old and threadbare. He was reluctant to throw it away, so he said he hung it at a strategic place where he would always see it so that he could always remember Papa. His interest in me was just that I was Papa Akindayomi's son. He prayed for me, blessed me and said Papa was an unforgettable blessing to him. That kind of experience can be multiplied many times over. Blessings I can't explain and which obviously I have not worked for come my way just like that.

Whenever I reflect on these things I realise it's because of my father's ways. And my own personal lesson from that is this: do good to anyone that you're opportune or privileged to help. Don't bother to look at how or when or if they would be paying you back. Most times it is not the people you help that help you back and most importantly what you've done comes back, often not to you, but to your children. My present car was a gift from a friend. He took me to his car pool and asked me to pick whichever one I liked. My landlord at my office, an elderly man, is a total stranger to me, but he just took especial interest in me and is always kind to me. I can't explain his love for me.

I went to bid for a job somewhere recently and a member of the panel asked if I knew Papa Akindayomi, *(people tell me I look like Papa)*. On learning that Papa was my Dad, this man overruled all other bids and gave the job to me. I see that till today, Papa's reservoir of prayer and good works are still following the children. I am a witness to the fact. Sometimes people want to be reluctant in doing good because they want payback. But from Papa's example, I believe it is God that pays back, and it may necessarily not be to you, but to your seed. So I always look forward to opportunities to show kindness to other people. I have learned from Papa's example.

PAPA AND PASTOR E. A. ADEBOYE
LIKE DAVID AND JONATHAN

The love and attachment between the two of them was incredible. Pastor Adeboye had his own room in our house. But despite that, any time he was around, himself and Papa would be locked away in Papa's room all day fasting, praying and obviously sharing all kinds of deep things. Even Mama could not drag them out to come and eat. To my mind there are things about Papa that even none of us his children knows but Pastor Adeboye alone. They were inseparable.

That Tulsa (Oklahoma) prayer you heard about was indeed the cry of the Spirit. Power was transferred excellently from that generation to the present one. It is believed that Pastor Rathod was one of the men that joined Papa to pray for Pastor Adeboye on this occasion.

Probably being Papa's last child, and being quite young when Papa passed away, Daddy E. A. Adeboye's love, kindness and concern for me and my family have been tremendous. I believe that the covenant love between him and Papa has extended to me too in a very special way.

I thank God for his faithfulness and commitment to Papa and his ideals.

CHAPTER EIGHT

'YE ARE WITNESSES OF THESE THINGS'

Luke 24: 48

Ile mi l'oke l'o wa/2x
Ma ma je n f'aye borun je
Ile mi l'oke l'o wa

B Y INTERPRETATION THAT SONG SAYS *my home is in heaven. Let me not live on earth in a way that spoils heaven for me.* A very special song to Papa Akindayomi all his life, but it became especially dearer to him after his first "death" experience when he was turned back at the very precincts of heaven. Until the very last moment when he finally went to be with the Lord Papa never tired of singing that song whether to his congregation or while busy at his many other assignments.

His final days were spent in bed rest. At this period Papa was said to have become more approachable and somehow tolerant of human frailties in people around him. Papa also spent this time re-emphasising some of the issues he had always harped upon to his people. This he told them was because God would not compromise on holiness and right standing, neither will He respect a person's church title. Papa was ever conscious of mortal man's inevitable accountability before God.

INCREDIBLE PROPHECIES
Right from the *"Ogo Oluwa" Prayer Society* days, Papa Akindayomi had been established as a highly prophetic man of God. Even supposedly mundane issues as employment, owning properties, etc were not too trivial for Papa to give a word about. And not that he would speak from his emotions or natural mind, but accurately from the mind of God. It did not seem to matter to him if the person he was giving the word was the exact opposite of what he told them. Some even looked like they could never in a lifetime come near that which the man prophesied to them about. But he would give the word anyway, and often it came to pass.

As it was in the beginning, where it was written for our own admonition that our elders in the faith, even when they were quite far from what God had said about them, chose to be persuaded and so embraced God's promises; we read their stories today that they became exactly what God had said. The whole matter at stake when a believer confronts the prophet's ministry is the issue of believing. For indeed if you believed you would act in certain ways that would see you truly becoming. The poor, indigent widow of Zarepath only had to believe the word of prophet Elijah, and the prophet's pronouncement worked for her.

The story was told of a certain brother Matthew who was faced with compound problems: unable to pay school fees, thrown out by his elder brother; and other matters. Brother Matthew found alternative accommodation in some slum area of Yaba. The place was your equivalent of John Bunyan's *"Valley of Despond."* The structure was a precarious all planks affair in deplorable conditions and no flooring at all. Water constantly seeped through the rough earth. But the brother stayed there for years struggling just to make ends meet.

One day out of the blues, Papa Akindayomi just showed up at the place. He had been visiting around the area and decided to call on brother Matthew also, because you see, Papa was a lover of people. Calling from the entrance, Papa asked, *"where is the landlord in this place?"* The fellow who was at the back of the building heard the greeting but did not respond. He could not see himself even as a tenant of a decent place in light years ahead. So why should he answer? *Landlord?* You must be joking! It sounded too far-fetched to register in his mind. He could barely afford the pittance for that wretched place. So despite being the only one at home brother Matthew did not answer Papa's greeting.

When he got no response, Papa entered the house and peeped around until he saw his host. Promptly he said, *"brother Matthew, but I had been calling you!"* The young man looked at Papa blankly: *"Yes, you. Don't you know you're the one I'm calling landlord?"* The young man greeted the old man respectfully, but displayed no emotion. However, the appellation *"landlord"* stuck among brother Matthew's friends and no one hardly knew him by his real name anymore.

Eventually this brother Matthew *(who eventually became a Pastor in RCCG)* had such a drastic turn around that over time he became owner of very many houses in decent parts of Lagos. Stories of such encounters with Papa could be multiplied severally in different aspects of life. Right at that smelly lagoon front, with his corp of the faithful, Papa Akindayomi with the unction of God's Spirit spoke forth the promises the Lord gave him concerning the new church named the Redeemed Christian Church of God. Nobody could have believed such prodigious pronouncements looking at the little band of barely literate people, being led by the former white garment prophet who was completely unlettered! But the man spoke forth anyhow, and the look on his face never suggested to anybody that the man was joking.

Even if nobody else believed him, Akindayomi believed himself because he knew his God so well. That, no one could doubt. And today, as many as have either heard of RCCG, or been active members or friends and associates of the church, are witnesses of these things:-
1)   The name of the church shall be:
       The Redeemed Christian Church of God.
       The church still bears the name till today.

2) His successor shall be a man about his height and build, using the same suit size as he and more learned than himself. Papa repeated this prophecy to the church for very many years before Pastor Adeboye ever showed up at all.

- The first day Dr. E. A. Adeboye came to the Ebute - Metta church *(for very different reasons altogether)*, without having met the new comer personally, Papa told his people, *"my successor is now here with us."*

Even though Pastor Adeboye greatly resisted such call of God upon his life, but today he is the General Overseer of The Redeemed Christian Church of God. As God's assignment became clearer and clearer to him, the young man of God dropped his impressive academic title of Dr. and embraced the humble appellation of Pastor (Enoch Adejare Adeboye).

3) That white people would worship God at RCCG, and that Akindayomi would witness it:
- In the year 1980, Papa had the joy of ordaining a Canadian by the name of Pastor Stephen Rathod. Rathod was said to have told Papa that God told him to come to Nigeria and ask Papa Akindayomi to ordain him and become his spiritual father. Till today Pastor Steve Rathod still attends RCCG's national Holy Ghost Congress here in Nigeria.

Since after Papa's death, countless foreigners (*worshippers and ministers*) have been coming and going, especially during RCCG special programs like the popular Holy Ghost Congress and the Annual Convention.

4) That RCCG would become a worldwide phenomenon: the specific word given to Papa Akindayomi was, "**prepare a people for the Lord...**"

- Since RCCG's formal launching in Lagos, Nigeria, it has virtually gone round the present world as we know it today with vibrant branches and mission fields in both remote and visible parts of Africa, Asia, the Americas, Europe, North America, the Arab world and India. And the church is still spreading.

Right now RCCG has registered its presence in Saudi Arabia.

In 1995, the first edition of the RCCG International Directory was launched, to assist travelers (*local and international*) find a place of worship anywhere in the world. The most current is the 2005 updated edition which contains names, addresses, telephone numbers and other useful information about RCCG parishes worldwide.

The prophet is gone but as it was revealed unto him that not unto him alone, but also unto his seed did he prophesy these things, we are his witnesses today. The Spirit of Christ is still present today to confirm that these things were indeed from the beginning.

5) That the Lord would still meet RCCG standing on earth at His second coming.
- In the doctrines, practice, sermons and activities of the RCCG, as led by the present General Overseer (Pastor E. A. Adeboye), the church is making all efforts to remain a ready Bride whenever the Bridegroom would show up.

"MY SON, HEARKEN TO MY VOICE"
"Howbeit that was not first which is spiritual but that which is natural; and afterward that which is spiritual" - I Corinthians 15: 46

Never one to reckon much with physical ailments *(although he was not given to sickness)* , but towards the end of his life Papa Akindayomi showed visible signs of tiredness and fatigue. His body had taken much punishment and pummeling throughout his earthly sojourn and had been made to serve him as optimally as possible. While Papa was grateful to God for the much he could get done here on earth, he had tender words of advice for his sons in the faith as his own physical strength ebbed away.

Papa told his sons that inasmuch as fasting and subduing the flesh was good for spiritual ministry and victory they should not so overdo it that they end up abusing their bodies. In his early days, it had been poverty and lack that, to an extent, dictated his diet even though he was given to much fasting and praying. But Papa admonished his successors in the work of the Lord that whenever they went on long fasts they should take time to nourish their bodies back to health and good living: take lots of fruits, eat choice foods to replenish lost body nutrients and rest properly. Papa told them that these things were necessary in order to prolong life, ensure good health and attain optimum effectiveness in the spiritual assignment.

As if to corroborate Papa's final fatherly advice and establish its universal application, American preacher and evangelist, Kenneth Copeland while celebrating thirty years of ministry documented the following observation. It's about his mother:-

> I don't like to think about where I would have ended up if my mother had not laid down her life for me in prayer. I was headed for hell as fast as I could go. But mother would get in prayer sometimes and stay there for days and days.
> "Daddy," I asked one time, "doesn't Mama ever sleep?"
> "Son," he said, "she never even wrinkles the sheets."
> The doctors told her when she was about 30 years old that she wouldn't live. They

told her the same thing when she was 40. *"You will never live another 10 years,"* they said when she was 50.

She lived all right, but she spent her life praying like she was going to die. She'd pray all night long. She prayed all the time. She'd pray... pray...pray. She later said when she was in her 70's, *"If I'd known I was going to live so long, I would have taken better care of myself."* [1]

And this, beloved, is Papa Akindayomi's last admonition to as many as have been privileged to be partakers of his spiritual heritage. While performing our spiritual responsibilities, we do not have to neglect the care of our earthly tabernacle alongside, for this is indeed the house of the spirit-man.

THE MAN DIED!

According to Papa Akindayomi's erstwhile driver, Pastor Z. A. Mulero, many of them around Papa thought people like him never slept nor stayed at all on this planet earth overnight. *"We used to think they went back to heaven at night and returned from there in the morning, just like the angels of God. It was unthinkable to assign mortal deeds to them."* But really it is not so. It is just the commitment and passion that set men like this one apart from regular mortals.

But then every man is mortal after all. The first sting of death from Eden as a result of the original sin would still take its toll. This particular flesh that had tasted sin would still submit to the laws of corruption. But eternal death is not the portion of the true believer in Christ. The Bible says, **"But if the Spirit of Him who raised Jesus dwell in you, He who raised Christ from the dead will also give life to your mortal bodies through His Spirit who dwells in you"** (Romans 8:11 NKJV).

So there it is. We shed mortality now so that we might put on immortality at the resurrection. We put the body of sin away that the soul might transit to heaven. With the resurrection body it is then raised in newness and immortality and incorruption, according to the Word of God. That Jesus resurrected is our hope, assurance and confidence that we would also resurrect at the last trump of God.

And this is the reason why, for the true believer death is never cessation of existence but actually a transition from one level of living to a higher and better level. Apostle Paul says, **"There is one glory of the sun, another glory of the moon, and another glory of the stars; for one star differs from another star in glory. So also is the resurrection of the dead. The body is sown in corruption, it is raised in incorruption. And as we have borne the image of the man of dust, we shall also bear the image of the heavenly Man"** (I Corinthians 15:41-42, 49 NKJV).

In the fashion of the fathers, right from father Abraham, Papa Akindayomi did not die *"suddenly"* or *"untimely"* as they say it in the world. No, never. He was ready and fully prepared when death came. Death is our horse, and Papa rode it home gloriously. **"Death where is thy sting?"**

The man died full of years with great expectation of reward and glory. Papa Akindayomi finished strong and left triumphantly in the breaking hours of Sunday, November 2nd, 1980.

Present were his wife (now) late Mama Esther Egbedire Akindayomi, Pastor (Mrs.) Folu Adeboye, and other church elders and pastors.

Glory to God!

<u>NOTES</u>
1) **Kenneth Copeland Publications:**
   The First 30 Years: A Journey of Faith
   (Fort Worth, Texas. 1997) : 13

SOLEMN WARNINGS FOR THE FUTURE

WHEN THE LORD JESUS HAD FINISHED His own assignment of birthing the Church with His blood, He handed over the baton to the rest of His able apostles whom the Bible says had been witnesses of both His suffering and also His glory.

The Lord gave great promises concerning the future of the Church on earth, but He did not neglect to sound sober warnings too concerning where the Apostles should particularly watch out for the enemy.

Apostle Paul told the church at Jerusalem, with tears in his eyes that: **"For I know this, that after my departing shall grievous wolves enter in among you, not sparing the flock. Also of your own selves shall men arise... Therefore watch, and remember...."** (Acts 20: 29-31).

So also in the pattern of the first Son of God, and in true

Apostolic tradition, Rev. J. O. Akindayomi also mentioned areas of concern as the Lord showed them to him where the coming generations of the RCCG family should beware; namely:-

1) The Quest and Ambition for Position

Papa said RCCG in future would be so powerful and influential that along with the faithful many others would stream in whose all-consuming passion would be to gain prominence, and position. He said such ones should beware, because RCCG belongs to the Lord and that was why he himself had said the church did not belong to him and whether he was there or not the church would prosper. But the ambitious ones should beware.

2) Money

Papa Akindayomi made his people to understand that despite that the future wealth of RCCG was also guaranteed, yet they should take care that money and the love of it do not become their focus.

At the start of the church Rev. Akindayomi suffered such heart-rending poverty and privation that at a point it became difficult even for some of his very close aides to continue with him. They left. Yet in spite of that, the man of God was most selective of gifts of cash, cars, and even lands. His main focus was pleasing the Lord and building according to the pattern given him.

This is why RCCG has survived the storms and continues to blossom and thrive, expanding the frontiers greatly.